THE MAYORS' INSTITUTE
EXCELLENCE IN CITY DESIGN

National Endowment for the Arts

Washington, DC

The Mayors' Institute on City Design

James S. Russell editor
Mark Robbins series editor

Distributed by:
Princeton Architectural Press
37 East Seventh Street
New York, New York 10003

For a free catalog of books, call 1.800.722.6657.
Visit our web site at www.papress.com.

Design by M. Christopher Jones, The VIA Group LLC.

Printed and bound in the United States of America.

Library of Congress Cataloging-In-Publication
Data is available from the National Endowment
for the Arts.

ISBN 1-56898-377-8

NEA Series on Design

Other titles available in this series:

Schools for Cities:
Urban Strategies

Sprawl and Public Space:
Redressing the Mall

University-Community
Design Partnerships:
Innovations in Practice

Your Town:
Mississippi Delta

Front cover:
Queensborough Public
Library, Flushing, New
York; The Polshek
Partnership, architect
Photo: © Jeff Goldberg/Esto

Contents

Preface

Mark Robbins
Director of Design, National Endowment for the Arts

The multiple disciplines of design—architecture and landscape architecture, graphic, fashion, and industrial design, planning and preservation—have long been a component of funding at the National Endowment for the Arts. Diverse programs serve varied constituents through support for design innovations, community charettes, master plans, and design competitions. As part of the Arts Endowment's mission to strengthen communities, NEA grants and special initiatives fund architects and designers, critics and historians, as well as the publications, lectures, conferences, and museums and galleries that bring their work to a broader public. These projects reach from Bozeman, Montana, to Birmingham, Alabama, to New York City and Los Angeles.

Design professionals are clearly aware of their disciplines' profound impact on the quality of the public realm and realize that their participation can be critical in shaping the ways cities and communities are conceived and built. Outside of the field, however, recognition of design's key role in the formation of cities, infrastructure, and public space is more limited. A series of initiatives by the design discipline of the NEA seeks to address this chronic situation, enhancing understanding of design among political leaders and the public.

One such program is the Mayors' Institute on City Design (MICD), founded in 1986 as an NEA Leadership Initiative. The MICD offers a forum that brings mayors from across the county together with design professionals to provide information about urban design that is comprehensible and encourages action. Since its inception the MICD has provided design resources for over 600 mayors of American cities. Design may not seem an obvious option for mayors grappling with the rigors of city governance. Yet every day they address issues that an understanding of design could usefully inform: economic and community development, zoning and other regulations, housing and transportation. The MICD's goal is to give mayors the expertise to become advocates for design, better attuned visually and practically to development opportunities and pitfalls. As stewards for their cities, they recognize that design can be a powerful tool.

Recent efforts to broaden the impact of the MICD program have resulted in partnerships with other federal agencies, helping to secure broader conversations between elected officials and the agencies that have an impact on the public environment. These partnerships have generally focused on a particular topic, such as brownfields reclamation in a collaboration with the Environmental Protection Agency. The General Services Administration, the nation's landlord, partnered with the NEA for an MICD addressing the impact of federal building projects on city centers. The Department of Housing and Urban Development has collaborated on sessions directed at encouraging housing in the downtown core, using innovative approaches for the design of denser neighborhoods.

Cities are the biggest and most complex things that we make as a society, and each city is unique with its own character, strengths, and potential. Consequently, there is no one instant solution (a stadium, an entertainment zone, a pedestrian mall) that can be applied universally and uncritically. We must not replace one orthodoxy with another regarding the city plan, nor reduce our thinking to issues of style or taste. In a rush for a believable urban center, a city cannot remake itself into a vision of the last century but must value historic buildings and spaces of all periods while also encouraging innovative new building solutions.

Unless we can understand new models for making cities and suburbs that incorporate the way we live—complete with big box stores and cars, as well as pedestrians—we will continue to perpetuate the kind of ill-considered commercial development one mayor of a western city termed his "sacrifice zone." Pre-existing models have lessons but without transformation cannot accommodate forms, land uses, building types, and a culture that have never existed before. Accommodating the car and the pedestrian and retail and residential spaces with reasonable densities requires careful thought. The Mayors' Institute is dedicated to fostering such thinking among both community leaders and design practitioners. To this end, the MICD brings mayors in contact with the brightest, most progressive thinkers and design practitioners the nation has to offer.

In recent years the NEA has introduced other new Leadership Initiatives to nurture design talent and help improve the overall quality of design across the country. The New Public Works program sponsors national design competitions for public building and landscape projects. Other initiatives have focused on possibilities for reworking out-of-date suburban malls, revitalizing communities through the design of schools, and enhancing the quality of life in rural areas. These initiatives are part of a concerted effort by the NEA to develop public awareness about design, serve all the design disciplines, and act as a conduit for design expertise for local governments and federal agencies, perhaps the largest consumers of design. In concert, these NEA programs seek to encourage the engagement of design professionals in important sectors of our culture. Support for the production of design that is aesthetically and materially rich, technologically innovative, economical, and socially active must be within our reach as a nation.

Mayor Joseph P. Riley, Jr., of Charleston, South Carolina, initially envisioned the MICD's unique program idea, working in concert with Adele Chatfield-Taylor, my predecessor at the NEA. Both merit acknowledgment for their perceptive belief in design. The MICD has had a consistent and far-reaching impact on elected officials and American cities. Recognition is also due to Christine Saum, who in her role as Executive Director of the Mayors' Institute has shepherded this program with great dedication and managed many vital aspects of the production of this publication. Editor James S. Russell has brought both his eloquence and insight to the endeavor. Christine, Jim, and I have worked

as a team to frame the book, ably assisted by graphic designer
M. Christopher Jones of The VIA Group. We thank essayists Robert
Campbell, Richard Sennett, Allan Jacobs, Donovan D. Rypkema, Alex
Krieger, and Rosalie Genevro for their persuasive and stimulating
comments. We also express appreciation to all those who have provided
visual materials, as well as to Casius Pealer, who kept those materials so
well organized. At the Princeton Architectural Press, Kevin Lippert,
Jennifer Thompson, and Clare Jacobson have offered guidance and
support. Kristina Alg, the NEA's Graham Fellow in Federal Service,
has provided invaluable coordination of this volume and others in the
NEA design series.

Thanks are also due to all the designers and other resource per-
sonnel who have dedicated time and energy to serving on the MICD's
intensive three-day sessions. They are among our best advocates for
design and make the case for it at the most direct level. We hope that
this publication provides examples of the best practices nationally for
architecture, landscape architecture, and the other design disciplines.
The work of these design professionals affects crucial decisions that have
an impact on the way the public realm is used today and the way it will
accommodate the future.

The History of the Mayors' Institute

Christine Saum

"I have often said that I am the chief urban designer of my city," wrote Joseph P. Riley, Jr., the mayor of Charleston, South Carolina, to his friend Jaquelin Robertson, who was then dean of the School of Architecture at the University of Virginia. "I have many opportunities to affect proposed developments…making them better for the city or allowing them to be ordinary—or worse." In this 1985 letter, he asked Robertson if there was not some way a program could be devised to give mayors a more sophisticated understanding of how design could be used to improve the quality of both public and private development. He wanted to give mayors the tools to evaluate design and to proactively become involved with it as a tool to improve the scale, diversity, and livability of the built environment the city is responsible for creating or encouraging.

The two presented the idea to Adele Chatfield-Taylor, then the Director of Design Arts at the National Endowment for the Arts, who agreed to fund it as one of the Arts Endowment's Leadership Initiatives. Over the next few months, the format was developed and refined, and the first Mayors' Institute session took place at the University of Virginia in October 1986. The energizing effect of putting designers and mayors in the same room together, apart from the day-to-day concerns of running a city, was immediately evident. The national institutes have met twice yearly since then. In 1990, four regional institutes were established to increase outreach to a wider range of cities in the Northeast, Southeast, Midwest, and West. MICD continues to be funded by the NEA as a Leadership Initiative but is now carried out in partnership with The U.S. Conference of Mayors and currently administered by the American Architectural Foundation.

One participant, Daniel Kemmis, who was mayor of Missoula, Montana, when he participated in an MICD institute, called it "healing work." He added, "In almost every problem brought to the Mayors' Institute, you have the opportunity to make the city more whole, not only in a physical way but in the way that you involve your citizens. You have an opportunity to heal the civic structure itself."

How to Use the Mayors' Institute on City Design

Robert Campbell

The Mayors' Institute on City Design has been such a rich and diverse experience for so many people that it's hard to sum up a single purpose. But one goal is clear: it exists to encourage mayors to think of themselves as the designers of their cities. Nobody else, we would argue, is designing the American city. A lot of people are designing parts of it. Planners do that, and so do architects and traffic engineers and public works departments and developers and preservation groups and many others. But no one can put together the whole picture in any city quite the way the mayor can. Mayors have a unique opportunity. MICD helps them seize it.

The Case Study Approach

MICD sessions are organized around case-study problems. Each mayor presents a problem from his or her city for the other mayors and designers to discuss. Finding a solution isn't necessarily the goal. Urban design is a lengthy process that usually can't be resolved in a brief session. The real goal is for mayors and designers to learn from one another. Mayors observe how designers approach a problem, what values they emphasize, and what parallel cases they have experienced. Designers learn how cities are seen by their mayors, who must take into account the full human richness of city life with its multiplicity of issues and constraints. More often than not, mayors and designers turn out to agree on the important issues. As a result, mayors often go home feeling encouraged to trust their own urban design instincts in the face of the many pressures with which they must deal.

In the more than 15 years during which the MICD has existed, the case study problems have exemplified the full range of issues that can fall under the heading of "city design" or "urban design." Should a historic building be demolished—or preserved? Would a new monorail help the downtown? How about a pedestrian street? Or a pedestrian skyway? Or an in-town shopping mall? What about the declining central business district? How can you control growth—or stimulate it? And so on.

The MICD takes on some pretty small problems. We've talked about the best way to design sidewalks and how to expand a public library. It also takes on big issues, the ones that tend to recur, such as the problem of public access to the waterfront. Big or small, all are urban design and all are important. Such issues land on the desk of America's mayors every day. We read of them in newspapers and see them on television. At MICD sessions, mayors get a chance to work with some very experienced urban designers in thinking about these issues.

A city in Iowa is worried about a shopping center, including a Wal-Mart store, that is proposed for a site three miles out of town. It will bring jobs and money to the region. It may make shopping more convenient. But what will it do to Main Street? And if Main Street fails, what happens to the city's character, its awareness of history, its pride in its identity? Does a remote shopping mall nurture a sense of community as well as does a central Main Street? What about the cosmic design issues—pollution and sprawl and the survival of the planet? The city is right to be concerned. What is the best solution?

A city in Missouri hopes to build a new convention center to "stanch the bleeding of jobs and business across the state line." But another city, Washington, D.C., finds that its new convention center is a mixed blessing. It has driven up real-estate values around it to the point at which small retailers, who it was hoped would benefit from it, are instead being forced out of business. Are convention centers a good idea? Where are they best located? How should they be designed?

The mayor of a state capital—stimulated as it happens, by a session of the MICD—proposes height limits on all new buildings in the area of the capitol building, so that the building's dome can continue to rise symbolically above the world of commerce. Opponents argue that lowering heights may push healthy economic growth out of town. Who is right? Can growth be accommodated in low-rise buildings? Are design controls a good idea? How do you write and enforce them?

Prince Charles of Great Britain argues that modern architecture is too often ugly and we should go back to the more humane qualities of older styles of building. Is this merely elitist nostalgia? Or are there lasting truths we can learn from the patterns by which buildings and cities were put together in the past? The media raise issues like these, but often without perceiving the implications of urban design. The MICD instead considers design questions when viewing civic decisions.

A Word About Values

The MICD doesn't push any particular dogma about how to design cities. Instead, it assumes that the mayors and the faculty designers know cities best and should be left alone to learn from one another. Nevertheless, there is an underlying belief that urban centers—from small towns to metropolises—are good places to live and work. That belief is sometimes challenged in our society today.

The MICD believes, too, that cities needn't just happen. They can and, in general, should be designed. If nobody is designing them, they become the chaotic and accidental result of a random collision of forces. Design doesn't mean, of course, imposing anybody's single vision. It means working through the democratic process toward a consensus view of what the shape of the city should be.

We also maintain that a city isn't something that can be understood by charts and statistics alone. A city is a physical thing that you have to engage with your senses. To understand it you have to see and hear and smell and touch it, move through it, watch how people use and cope with it. The physical city is billboards and trees and waterways, boarded-up shop fronts and sparkling new boutiques, abandoned rail yards and gleaming office towers, handsome streets and asphalt deserts, historic homes and fast-food restaurants, traffic jams and bus routes, street patterns that work and others that don't.

Mayors spend much of their time dealing with aspects of the city that are abstract rather than physical—taxes, budgets, and economic and social issues of all kinds. All are important, and all interact with urban design. But urban design itself—the shaping of the physical city as a setting for the life of its inhabitants—is the emphasis of the MICD.

Robert Campbell, FAIA, is a practicing architect, educator, and author in Boston. His work as architectural critic for the *Boston Globe* was recognized in 1996 with the Pulitzer Prize for Distinguished Criticism.

I

The Disciplines

1

3

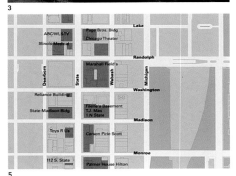

2

4

5

1
A glass pavilion opens
onto a Reading Garden at
the Allston Branch of the
Boston Public Library.
Machado and Silvetti
Associates, architect

2
A curve of stone steps
defines a quiet place next
to the White River at the
Central Indianapolis
Waterfront Capital City
Landing. Sasaki
Associates, landscape
architect and urban
designer

3
A "park" that advertises
its artificiality defines a
student gathering place in
New York City's West Side
High School. Ellen and
Allan Wexler, artists

4
St. Paul on the Mississippi,
a development framework,
guides the future of downtown. Berridge Lewinberg
Greenberg Dark Gabor
Limited, urban planner

5
Restoring vibrancy to
State Street, in Chicago,
included the strategic
targeting of aid to
individual properties.
Skidmore Owings &
Merrill, urban designer

The Design Professions

James S. Russell

Any endeavor with "design" in its name can seem mystifying because it unites artistic creativity with problem solving and technological savvy. A public official or agency head usually is more comfortable discussing quantifiable issues ("we need 10 more classrooms here") or the technical side, because issues and criteria are objective. The intuitive side of design, in which designers use style and aesthetics to express an entire community's culture and ideals, can seem a difficult subject for public consideration. Officials may fear that no single design can ever reconcile the community's varying aspirations and preconceptions. One of the main reasons the MICD has been so successful is that it helps mayors understand how the subjective and objective threads of thinking are united by the designer, and it also helps them speak to constituents and colleagues about the benefits of design at the highest level.

To satisfy the quantifiable aspect of a project, the designer works to make sure that spaces relate properly to each other or that people can easily find their way through an urban square. Thousands of additional decisions must also be made. What finishes that will be durable yet still inviting can be used in a library? How should a stadium be placed so that it seems to extend the city rather than lie isolated in a sea of parking?

Resolving the functional issues of a project should be considered a baseline, something you should expect from any competent, experienced designer. It is common to think that designers solve the pragmatic issues then "add the aesthetics." But a high-quality work of architecture isn't a box full of rooms wrapped in a pleasing package. A piece of public art does not become meaningful if it is only decorative. The "art" of design is the synthesis of aesthetic *and* functional issues—of beauty *and* meaning.

The intuitive side of the designer's brain is often the side that drives the designer's passion to do his or her best. There's an alchemy available there to create a memorable public work that can emotionally connect to the community and be embraced by it.

What Should You Expect of a Designer?

Aspiring to the highest quality of design can mean rewriting the project script somewhat. The designer may question given circumstances rather than accept them automatically. Is this the right site? Doesn't this program miss an important issue? Does this project successfully anticipate future growth? Sometimes a questioning, creative approach makes itself felt more prosaically: If two public health agencies shared one reception area, rather than each having a separate one, couldn't you have a single, more welcoming reception area?

A successful work of design looks like it belongs, which means that, in any of a variety of ways, the designer has figured out what is unique about the setting that can be expressed or brought forward in the project. A work of design is distinctive when it integrates and transforms the given circumstances so that they make a sum that is greater than the parts. Design expresses the values of its community to the people that use a building or just pass it by. A neighborhood library can look like a fortress, conveying the idea that the city has given up, or that it is only for those invited, or who are willing to do what it takes to breach its defenses. Or a library can be welcoming, a beacon suggesting that struggle against decline has its reward, a place for meeting and socializing, as well as for quiet reading and research.

Public officials in charge of a building program are responsible to a budget and to a wide array of "publics," many of whom have highly specific agendas. The path of least resistance can be to divvy up the project into bits that please this or that constituency. The resulting building can look like the cobbled-together evidence of the public passions of the moment, speaking to the contentions of urban life rather than to the many possibilities that unite us. Officials should not hesitate to use a good designer's integrative artistic bent to reconcile controversial aspects of a project. Very often people exposed to the other interests exerting pressure on a project will recognize that there are numerous ways to proceed.

Officials should encourage the designer to create at the highest artistic level. People often fear innovative design simply because, in their experience, the new (compromised a dozen ways in a vain attempt to please everyone) has always been worse than the old. A creative design can often exceed expectations and win approval, even from those thought most likely to oppose it, especially if it expresses a serious effort to take every relevant concern into account.

On a political level, the designer can act as an independent third party, a person seen by conflicting factions as dedicated to finding the best resolution and who can be an honest broker. A designer, planner, or artist dedicated to serving the public will try out alternate approaches to a project to accommodate the desires of its users. The very act of creating alternatives often points the way to the best solution.

Judging Design Aesthetics

People tend to be most comfortable reviewing the objective qualities of design: Does it have the rooms we need in the sizes we requested? In an era of artistic pluralism, it can be hard for the public and for officials to judge whether architecture is aesthetically appropriate, or even beautiful. That the design is consistent or inconsistent with one's personal taste is not an adequate barometer. There are too many views of taste and style today; catering to one or another doesn't in itself guarantee a project that is embraced by the community and that won't seem dated in a very few years.

A designer may propose a solution that makes some people uncomfortable because it strays far from their own aesthetic sensibilities or does not seem to fit into the community. But design criteria that apply when decorating one's own home do not apply when one is creating a public building. Public places must find a means to express the idea of people coming together; they are not domestic environments.

Words like "dignity," "gravity," "welcoming," and "community" are often used to denote appropriateness for a public building. For some, this means embracing historical styles in which columns, entablatures, or domes denote a continuity with the past. Historical elements can more deeply resonate if they are integrated and interpreted, so that the scale and uses appropriate to modern life are not simply shoehorned into a historical-looking shell.

Continuity with history is not the only way to achieve appropriateness. Communities change, and design that recognizes and expresses a community's changing identity helps maintain a community's authenticity and sense of place. Indeed, so many places in America lack a specific sense of place that the public work created with a fresh palette of materials and forms can uncover its unique mélange of history, environment, and culture.

A useful stance in judging a design is to be open-minded but not hesitate to question or criticize. If the aesthetic evokes discomfort, don't hesitate to ask the designer to explain it further. If you don't understand the design, ask the designer to find ways (through drawings or models or through examples of similar designs) to enhance your understanding. Whether the aesthetic attempts to blend in or offers a unique counterpoint to its surroundings, there should be a rationale that is both comprehensible and sensible. Some ground rules apply in a public design process: The designer should gracefully receive feedback and respond to it in subsequent iterations. The citizen should recognize that not every project can be all things to all people, and try to judge the compromises the designer has made dispassionately.

In any project, decisions have to be made about keeping the project within the budget. Inevitably the desires of the community exceed the budget. Public projects are often more expensive, on a per-square-foot basis, than seemingly similar private sector projects. But public projects must contribute to, and make a statement about, their communities in ways private construction is not required to do.

Still, there are times when the project needs to be trimmed to meet the budget and times when the budget simply needs to be increased. It is a key responsibility of public staff and officials to know which applies in a given circumstance and to bite the bullet either way. Great design cannot salvage an inadequately budgeted project.

Design and construction schedules may also be contentious. Public structures should be erected to a realistic schedule consistent with that of other projects of similar scope and complexity. Since ideal schedules are not always possible, officials and the public must understand what may be traded away. A short schedule usually increases the cost of the project. It also risks unanticipated delays because barriers, in the form of public resistance or unexpected physical conditions on the site, have a way of sabotaging speed-driven projects. Great projects are sabotaged more often than not by rushing to get them done. It is too easy to forget that what we build today represents an investment in the public realm for a long time to come.

Once a schedule is understood and agreed to, the client should expect the design team to maintain that schedule. Although construction projects often seem to take longer than projected, no unjustified or unreasonable delay should be regarded as acceptable. If the scope of the project must be cut to achieve early occupancy, it should be understood by everyone involved so that the most intelligent decisions can be made.

In the struggle to meet budgets and timetables, it's important for officials and the community to keep in mind what's at stake. A mistake in the procurement of an ordinary service or product can almost always be corrected; a public work installed in the "get it done cheap and fast" mode will cast its dispiriting and dysfunctional shadow over a community for decades.

There are those who argue that public buildings should be procured and built to standards of private developers, but the development community today builds to maximize short-term profit and ignores high short- and long-term maintenance costs. These costs are unacceptable for a government agency that must hold a building for a long time. A building that represents the government agency to the public should express its community's aspirations and demonstrate a commitment to the community's future.

Hiring a Designer

Design is a professional service, not a commodity. Within any community, there is enormous variety in capability and quality of professional services available. That's why a quality-based selection process will almost always produce a superior, more cost-effective result over a fee-bid selection process. "Quality" can be understood and evaluated in a number of ways. The client should look for a comfort-inducing combination of experience and expertise, a record of pleasing past clients by delivering quality service on time and at reasonable cost, and a passion and commitment to achieving the best possible design.

In this book, each design discipline is considered separately, since most firms specialize in one area. Typically the architect, landscape architect, urban designer, planner, or artist assembles a team of specialized consultants suited to the project's requirements. But multi-discipline firms, such as an architect/engineer or a planner/landscape architect/urban designer, offer a wide range of design, engineering, and specialized services in-house (for example, lighting design, environmental-impact analysis, and traffic studies). Either approach has virtues: A team of independent consultants allows the community to hire the best practitioners in respective fields, with the mix of disciplines customized to the job at hand. Such an arrangement demands a commitment among the participating firms to excellent communication. The "one-stop shopping" multiservice firm approach is appealing for its convenience, and works well when there is a high level of expertise in each discipline, when appropriate disciplines are represented within the firm, and when internal communication is well integrated. For the decisionmaker, the quality of the menu of services offered under single-firm, multidiscipline leadership must be considered against the ability to customize a mix of services obtained independently from several independent firms.

The Architect

James S. Russell

In the simplest terms, architects design buildings. The contract between architect and client usually says that the architect creates a set of documents based on a program (the rooms, spaces, and functions that address the client's needs). From these documents, the contractor constructs the actual project. The best architects go far beyond drawing up workable floor plans, however. The experience of moving through a building can have drama or offer unexpected surprises. It can orchestrate informal, unexpected gatherings or encounters for the public. It can invite people who have not previously felt part of a community. Spaces within buildings can express a community's highest values like dignity, reconciliation, neighborliness.

The spaces required by the program can be arranged within an envelope that has a unique quality of its own, that deploys materials in an artistic way while keeping the rain out and the heat in. Expressive materials and detailing recognize what is special about a place, like a beautiful patina that develops on a surface over time thanks to the local climate. In the hands of a good architect, a site, however ordinary it may seem, is something with innate qualities that can be brought forth in an expressive way. Daylight is not just for illumination but has a beauty in its own right that changes with the seasons and that can be choreographed by the artful deployment of building openings.

Metreon is an emerging type of building, the urban entertainment center. Though it is inwardly focused, a kind of mall for electronic and cinematic entertainment, architect Simon Martin-Vegue Winkelstein Moris, with Gary E. Handel Associates, opens its several levels to dramatic public lobbies that draw passersby into the excitement of what goes on within. It takes advantage of crowds drawn to the adjacent Yerba Buena Gardens in San Francisco, a public and private initiative that includes a variety of cultural institutions, a park, and a children's center.

1

2

3

4   Photo: © Jeff Goldberg/Esto

5   Photo: © AlanKarchmer/Esto

6   Photo: © Jeff Goldberg/Esto

22

It can be useful to involve the architect in predesign services like site selection and program development. Determining financial feasibility and securing financing, however, is usually best left to specialists. It is rare for the architect to act as the contractor for a project, though standard professional agreements call for the architect to represent the public client during construction by monitoring that the design is executed properly by the builder. Many public projects are managed without the services of the architect during the construction phase, but this approach often works poorly because the officially appointed person in charge lacks the resources or knowledge of the architect. Some jurisdictions prefer to use a single entity to design and build the project. "Design/build" as a project-delivery method works best when the specific complexities of the project demand specialized construction expertise. Under such circumstances, the contractor can offer critical advice throughout the design process. In complex design/build projects, both the architect and the builder should be selected on the basis of quality and expertise, not on price alone.

A skilled architect combines excellent analytical capabilities, technical experience, and a deeply held aesthetic sensibility. The appropriateness of the latter quality can be the most difficult to gauge. We live in a particularly pluralistic era of architectural expressiveness. There is no "typical" style and a high degree of expressive individuality has developed, which, of course, can be confusing to communities trying to make a choice about the appropriateness of a design.

What style is right for a given project? Today, many architects work in a highly sculptural, expressionistic style. This design approach is probably best suited to difficult settings where making a strong aesthetic statement can create an identity where one doesn't exist or project an improved image for a troubled neighborhood. It can also be appropriate where the project or site presents unique conditions that deserve a special approach.

Another contemporary strain of design is the near opposite—a very discreet minimal and abstract approach that relies on careful proportions, elegant details, and impeccable use of materials. Such design is

Set within a park, the barnlike forms of the Heritage Park Community Center anchor a new planned community in Chula Vista, California. Rob Wellington Quigley Architecture/Planning, architect

often successful where the building needs to fit into a neighborhood: it can make a fresh, welcoming, contemporary statement. It is also suited to sites of unique quality or beauty; rather than draw attention to itself, it offers a quiet, strong statement as a counterpoint to the drama or beauty of the surrounding conditions.

A third design approach that communities often seek is a historicist style. Such designs use historical details or proportions to evoke an existing historic neighborhood or remind people of familiar historic images. This approach can succeed where there is a full and successful integration of the contemporary uses in the historically inspired envelope and where the scale of the program fits comfortably with historic proportions and details as well as the place within which the building is to be set. One of the reasons old buildings are pleasing is that they are built with an integrity endemic to their time and with a sense of materials and craft that is palpable. A historicist approach that does not aspire to the same integrity and execution of the structures it evokes will too often seem like stage-set history.

The Landscape Architect

James S. Russell

Landscape architecture has its roots in the design of parks and gardens. The profession has, however, extended its bounds considerably over the decades. Many landscape architects design such "hardscapes" as plazas, walkway systems, and other public environments, and their projects may range from zoo-viewing structures to playground equipment to outdoor paving systems. But the profession's traditional palette is landform, plantings, and water features—as well as the site's relationship to the local environment and climate. Since landscape architects may be well attuned to the local vagaries of climate, soils, vegetation, and topography, it is often useful to involve them in site selection or site evaluation.

While architects usually lead a project in which the landscape is subsidiary in complexity or cost to the building, landscape architects may lead a design team in park or open-space projects or when sites of significant environmental sensitivity are involved.

They may lead large multidiscipline firms or assemble independent consultants in various design and engineering disciplines to plan and design large greenbelt open spaces and lay out large-scale real-estate development projects. Working with planners and civil engineers, they may define strategies to apply to entire regions or ecosystems.

The growth of an environmental ethic has turned many landscape architects into shepherds of wild places, where "design" primarily means restoring that which the hand of man has damaged. Many are turning to

1

2

3

4

5

1
A former landfill in Palo Alto, California, Byxbee Park has become a work of art as well as a green refuge. Hargreaves Associates, landscape architect; Peter Richards and Michael Oppenheimer, artists

2
Special plants clean toxic soils at Ford Motor Company's River Rouge Plant, Dearborn, Michigan. D.I.R.T. Studio, landscape architect

3
The Central Indianapolis Waterfront Capital City Landing project has transformed nine miles of urban waterfront along Indiana's White River. A tangle of leftover spaces, and abandoned, environmentally degraded industrial sites has become a new focus of urban life. Instead of an unwanted "backyard," the waterfront has become the symbol of the city and a setting for new private investment. Sasaki Associates, landscape architect and urban designer

4
Fountains in a stone terrace suggest an array of stars at the Arthur Ross Terrace of the American Museum of Natural History in New York City. Kathryn Gustafson, landscape architect

5
"Ecliptic," at Rosa Parks Circle, a cooling fountain and pool in the summer, becomes an ice skating rink in the chill of the Grand Rapids, Michigan, winter. Maya Lin, architect, Quennell Rotschchild, landscape architect

"bioremediation" techniques to rescue polluted industrial brownfields for viable new uses. An emerging hybrid practice, "landscape urbanism," attempts to unite more seamlessly the disciplines of landscape architecture, architecture, and planning. In such firms, open-space consideration and pedestrian flows can more directly influence building design and road-and-bridge engineering.

The greater breadth of the discipline means that landscape architects find themselves competing with architects, planners, and urban designers, especially in complex, large-scale public projects. The question becomes how to choose. Matching the needs of the project to the specific experience and point of view of competing firms usually makes it easy to narrow the field to a few good contenders.

As in any profession, capabilities vary widely. But a job that requires specialized planting expertise (a severely degraded landscape or a garden of specimen plants) might better be handled by a trained horticulturist; garden maintenance is usually done by specialists in that field. While landscape architects may be involved in the design and even the contouring of large-scale land forms, it is usually civil engineers that design the irrigation and drainage systems, as well as other engineered infrastructure such as roads, for such landscapes.

Some landscape firms construct their own designs, but design/build may be appropriate only for the most specialized public projects. When a separate contractor is employed, landscape architects, like other design professionals, should act as the agent to the public client in assuring that the design is properly executed.

There is an enormous aesthetic diversity in landscape architecture today. In some firms, the work looks more sculptural; others seek a seamless integration between the landscape and freestanding structures or indoor spaces. Some firms prefer that the hand of the designer be nearly invisible; others are highly assertive. A given firm's aesthetic approach may closely dovetail with an ethic about the land. A clear understanding of that ethic and how it might be appropriate to the project at hand may aid the public agency in selecting the landscape architect.

The Urban Designer

James S. Russell

Urban design draws on the expertise in the planning and architecture professions in the physical design of urban environments. Three decades ago urban planning evolved away from the physical arrangement of urban realms toward a focus on social, demographic, and technical aspects of urban health. Urban design was born as architects and landscape architects sought to fill this gap and created academic programs that would prepare them to take on the complexities of neighborhood or community design. The urban designer, trained in both planning and architecture (though some are landscape architects), can design small public spaces or streets, entire neighborhoods, and even citywide or regional systems.

While urban designers may lay out an entirely new neighborhood or district, most are engaged in the revitalization of existing built-up areas. The "design" in the title correctly connotes an emphasis on establishing a desired quality, image, and identity, in physical form, but the endeavor seeks to solve functional issues at the same time. An urban-design scheme may address poor traffic circulation and poor connections between parts of the city. Another might lay out a brownfield site in lots and blocks to attempt to extend an existing adjacent neighborhood. Urban designers have reworked public housing projects and laid out new neighborhoods on abandoned military facilities. The urban designer's job may include laying out or reconfiguring streets and lots and organizing vehicular and pedestrian circulation and parking. Designers may prescribe new uses of space to augment those that exist in a neighborhood. They may determine the location and character of parks or natural reserves; offer detailed guidelines on building bulk, density, and form; lay out view corridors; or call for the preservation of key natural or manmade features. The urban designer sets the level of quality and amenities that will bind individual land owners, developers, and architects over the long term as the project is completed.

Often the urban designer's job is to work with citizens and elected officials to be sure key concerns are raised in a timely manner and addressed. Urban design inevitably involves elected officials who must understand what is being proposed and what the construction scenarios will mean.

The physical form of urban design is often informed by detailed studies of natural systems, transportation patterns, market studies, demographic and sociologic models, and local goals for diversity of users and incomes. Defining the scope of an urban-design project will determine what specialties must be present on the team. A neighborhood targeted for arts facilities, for example, may demand expertise in the performing-arts facility design or evaluation of the economics of publicly financed cultural facilities.

The work of urban design can be performed by firms that call themselves planners, landscape architects, or architects. While there are degree programs in urban design, there is not a licensure requirement (though most urban designers are licensed in another professional discipline). The client needs to consider carefully the capability and experience the problem at hand demands. A firm that specializes in urban design may be desirable, but an architecture firm may offer a unique design sensibility that suits the project requirements, while a landscape architecture firm may prove a better choice when a great number of environmental issues intrude. In many cases, all disciplines need to be represented.

Because urban design entwines a great number of public interests and private agendas, communication is key to its success. Urban designers deploy a number of means, such as visioning sessions, charettes, and

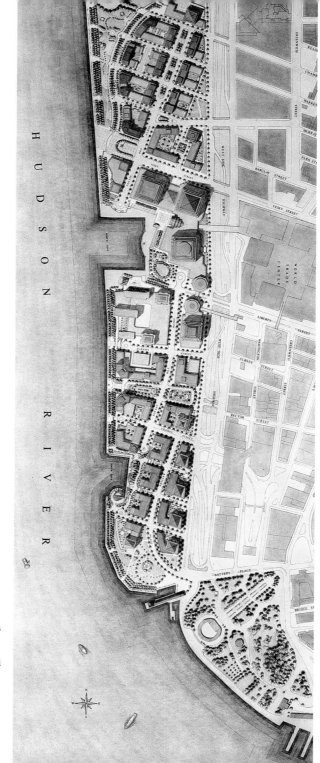

The master plan developed in 1979 for Battery Park City by Alexander Cooper Associates has guided construction on this vast landfill site, adjacent to New York City's financial district, for more than 20 years. Its extension of the city's traditional street grid and its fine grain have proven enormously influential.

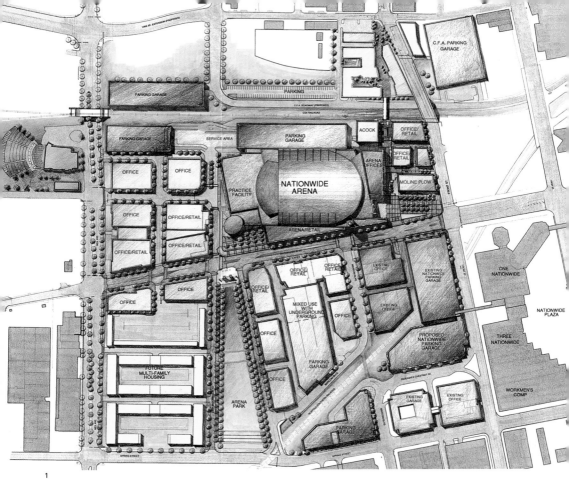

1

1

A sports stadium is the centerpiece of a new district at the edge of downtown Columbus, Ohio. Myers Schmalenberger/ MSI, with Sasaki Associates, master planners; Heinlein Schrock Sterns with NBBJ, stadium architects

2 / 3

The Cincinnati Riverfront Park wraps a historic bridge in a grand civic greensward. It unites two large sports stadiums along the river and opens a green front door to downtown. Hargreaves Associates, master planner

2

3

hands-on workshops (see "The Tools" section of this book), to help citizens and private interests foresee possibilities and understand the consequences of the choices the community makes.

In evaluating a firm's urban design work, it is important to consider the degree to which the firm has offered solutions tailored to the specifics of a situation. Be wary of guidelines that are either too loose (in which case the vitalizing strategy of a unique identity is lost) or too prescriptive (too costly or functionally inappropriate for compliance). The entities contracted to build out the plan must find it to be flexible and workable.

The urban designer must often make assumptions about a mix of uses or a configuration for given uses within a development. But circumstances change, and the designer's assumptions may not prove true over a long-time development process. An important measure of a design's success is its flexibility to accommodate evolving development economies.

The Urban Planner

James S. Russell

Urban planning came of age in the early 20th century, an era that placed great faith in science and technical professions to solve problems, including the perpetual obsolescence, inefficiencies, and unsanitary conditions that afflicted cities. The planner's job description was once to devise the plan that would guide the development of the entire city. But the work of planners has always been more diverse. Planners at various times have turned their attention to traffic flow, public order, aspects of city life that induce criminal and antisocial behavior, and overall quality of life. These days, planners may make plans for a downtown district or a residential neighborhood—or an entire region.

As the greater complexity of this endeavor has come to be recognized, planning has developed numerous subspecialties. Some are technical, such as analyses of transportation, environmental impact, and demographic change. Others are sociological: planners attempt to represent the aspirations of the many diverse populations that have a stake in the future of the city, sometimes representing citizens' groups directly (community-based planning), sometimes devising means to reconcile conflicting political agendas. Within city government itself, planners are usually responsible for managing the city's master planning document and for handling zoning changes and other regulatory tools that apply to urban development.

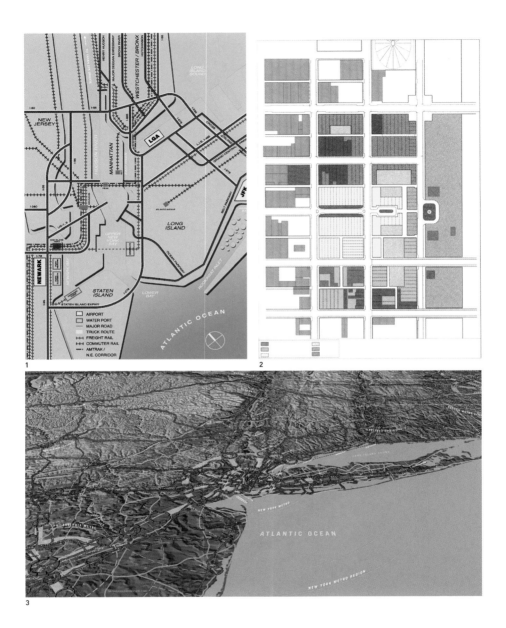

1

2

3

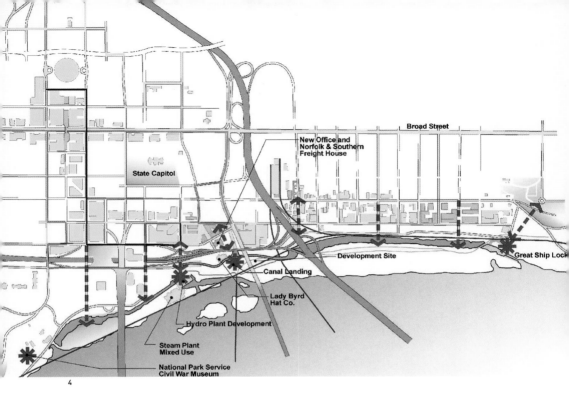

Broad Street

New Office and
Norfolk & Southern
Freight House

State Capitol

Development Site

Great Ship Lock

Canal Landing

Lady Byrd
Hat Co.

Hydro Plant Development

Steam Plant
Mixed Use

National Park Service
Civil War Museum

4

1
Solving transportation
problems around New
York City means analyzing
all modes at once. Michael
Gallis & Associates with
James S. Russell, plan-
ning and strategy

2
Resized streets and new
uses are bringing life back
to Albuquerque, New
Mexico's downtown. Moule
& Polyzoides, architects
and urbanists

3
The emerging form of
metropolitan New York
affects all the jurisdictions
it crosses. Michael Gallis
& Associates, planning
and strategy

4
Canal Walk used a historic
canal as an armature to
reconnect Richmond,
Virginia, with its riverfront.
Wallace Roberts & Todd,
planners

The tools of planning have become more various and sophisticated over the decades. Few cities rely on zoning alone anymore. The planning department may map a variety of special districts with specific requirements to maintain a certain character. Additional overlays may guard a district's historic qualities or require development techniques that preserve precious environmental characteristics. A variety of incentives may be deployed (ranging from tax abatements to permissions to create extra floor area) to encourage development. Planners may prioritize and guide public investment to strategic ends. While once planning dogma prescribed a careful separation of urban functions into districts pursuant to technologically deterministic criteria, today planners far more often orchestrate the mixing of compatible uses to assure economic diversity, quality of life, and a reliable tax base.

The role of planning is in some flux today. Many cities have dispensed with master plans, preferring to use planning strategically, to build on opportunities or create them. On the other hand, many cities dispensed with proactive planning along with their master plans, and now find they have neither the data nor the plans in place to react to opportunities, such as a short-term federal or state grant program for projects for which need has been established. Public officials, depending on budgetary realities and governing style, must decide how many planning functions should remain within government agencies and how many should be contracted to private professionals.

Urban design has taken on the physical design aspects of what planners once did. Environmental analysis specialists compete with traditional planners where environmental considerations are highest. Some planners have become pure community advocates, negotiating with government agencies to realize the aspirations of neighborhoods. Like urban designers, planners must be able to facilitate communication. Community involvement, interaction, and participation is critical to devising useful planning strategies and implementing them successfully.

Planning remains essential for a city to proactively realize its future in built form. No plan can do its job without the ongoing support and effort of the public officials charged with executing it.

The Artist

James S. Russell

The days when public art meant bronze heroes astride their rearing hors-
es are over. Art today finds its way into the public realm in ways as diverse
as the people it serves. Sculpture, whether figurative or abstract, is still
designed for lobbies, important public rooms, and plazas and parks.
Traditional media such as paintings, prints, and photographs often
enhance new public buildings. In addition, such ordinary elements of the
community landscape as retaining walls, lampposts, sidewalks, manhole
covers, bus shelters, sewage-treatment plants, and buses have become the
sites of well-received public art.

It is natural for the nonspecialist to feel intimidated by the sheer
diversity of methods and styles in art production today. The path to public art is not made easier by the occasional noisy controversies that have
arisen over specific pieces. The very passion public art can arouse, however, is important, because it testifies to how deeply people care about it.

Communities should not resist art that draws on deep emotions.
Art is capable of humanizing our streets and sidewalks. It can do this in
ways that enhance or heighten our sense of our surroundings, perhaps
challenging us to see those surroundings in a new way. Art can create or
express the uniqueness of a public place and enrich the larger cultural life
of a community by encouraging artistic production. How communities
hope to use public art is often key to determining the type of art that is

suitable to develop and also defining the criteria for artist selection.

Many public-arts advocates see the *process* of achieving a new work of art to be as important as the product. In a new school-building project, an artist may work with children to devise an expression of the community's history for other children to experience and learn from over the life of the building. Other artists make research or oral histories part of their design process in order to bring forgotten artifacts or entire landscapes alive in a contemporary way.

The means to acquire public art have widened in recent years. Much art is still commissioned by communities through percent-for-art programs, in which a fraction of a capital project's construction cost is set aside for the installation of art. Some communities require some provision for public art in projects by private developers, or ask developers to contribute to a public-art fund. Private owners or donors will often lend or give art to a community if the community will provide a suitable place to display it and make the commitment to maintain it. Public/private partnerships may make art for public places available on a rotating or temporary basis.

Since so much public art is procured as part of the process of altering or creating new buildings, parks, or other public works, one of the key questions public clients must ask is, "What is the role of the artist in the project?" For a lobby or plaza, a work of art may be selected or commissioned separately from the design of the building in which it is placed. Other projects seek to incorporate the art seamlessly, to the point, in some cases, where the line between the architect's work and the artist's is difficult for the viewer to determine. Getting the artist involved early in the process is a good way to ensure that the work does not appear to have been dropped onto the site as an afterthought. In park or greenbelt projects, the artists selected can often be landscape architects, sculpting landforms and "designing" wetlands to meet artistic and functional requirements. At an urban-design or planning scale, artists, architects, and industrial designers can create street furniture and sidewalk patterns, or substantially define the identity of a neighborhood through the design of a pedestrian bridge or neighborhood gateway.

Top:
The zipperlike Embarcadero Ribbon, though only a few feet wide, unifies a long stretch of the San Francisco waterfront because of its unique, arresting form. Stanley Saitowitz, architect, with Vito Acconci and Barbara Solomon, artists

Bottom:
A stream of water drips into The Water Room, a cooling place to pause along an irrigation canal path in Phoenix, Arizona. The water seeps under stones at the base of the room, offering a poetic form of natural air conditioning. M. Paul Friedberg, landscape architect; Jackie Ferrara, artist

1

2

3

4

5

6

A variety of models have developed to aid communities in selecting artists and works of art. For large art programs or citywide projects, an arts commission or similar body, usually aided by outside consultants, may devise a master plan that includes a description of how the community wants to use public art, its goals (such as making art a part of growing areas or focusing on stagnating or overlooked neighborhoods), and criteria for selection. These plans are often developed over a period of time with considerable public discussion as well as input from the local arts community. They can include guidelines and specify budget, location, and maintenance criteria.

For the acquisition of individual works of art, a community may make a broad call for submissions (inviting, essentially, any artist or designer to apply) or limit submission criteria. Some submittal processes are invitation-only. The work is best evaluated by a panel of recognized national or local art professionals augmented, as circumstances warrant, with a representative of the client or agency owner, community members, and elected officials.

1 / 2 / 3 / 4
Glass blocks containing local historical artifacts as well as objects solicited from embassies worldwide represent the range of the world's knowledge in tangible form at Stuyvesant High School, in New York City. "Mnemonics," Kristen Jones and Andrew Ginzel, artists

5 / 6
Engraved boxes urge students to drop in paper slips recording their own dreams and wishes. They are annually collated as a student-designed artwork at Walton High School, Bronx, New York. "Your Voices," Janet Zweig, artist

II

The Elements

The "Civitas" of Seeing

Richard Sennett

One problem in urban studies—probably the most vexing one—is how to see socially and morally. A city is not just a place to live, to shop, to go out, and to have kids play. It is a place that implicates the way in which people derive their ethics, how one develops a sense of justice, and, most of all, how we talk with and learn from people who are unlike ourselves—which is how a human being becomes human.

First, I will define what I mean by "public" as a social and moral term. "Public" meant to the ancient Greeks *synoikismos*, which is also the word for "making a city." The first part, *syn*, is a coming together, and the second, *oikos*, was a household unit in Greece, something between a family and a village—maybe the word "tribe" captures it—with its slaves and hangers-on. Greek cities were formed when these *oiki* migrated into a central place. This happened for two obvious reasons: as long as people were exposed out there on the Greek hills, they could be annihilated, and their economies never grew until people combined their energies.

What *synoikismos* denotes, however, is a peculiar problem. It not only describes putting people together functionally. The term literally means to bring together in the same place people who need each other but worship different household gods. The public problem for the Greeks was how people who needed each other functionally could live in the same place—even when they did not share the same values. It is a problem that persists in all Western cities: How can we let people live

Libraries have never been such a focus of community life as they are today. Browsers hunting a meaty novel (or a good CD) join parents who are introducing toddlers to reading, job-seekers who are brushing up on skills, and teenagers doing homework. Meeting rooms serve senior knitting circles during the day and AA meetings in the evening. The Polshek Partnership designed entry steps to signal welcome for the Queensborough Public Library in New York City.

47

together who worship different household gods? How do differing people find a way to use the word "we"?

Different People Sharing Public Space

The meaning of the word "public" has been pretty debased. The practical use of the term "public space" in cities, for example, connotes spaces where people go to buy things. We think about shopping malls, downtowns, and so on in terms of consumption and pleasure. Missing is any sense of the Greek notion of *polis*, which expresses something more consequent and political about the condition of people with differences being concentrated in the same place.

How do people learn from each other's differences? Most shopping malls depend on constant circulation of traffic. If people sit down for two or three hours, as they might in a Parisian café, and just talk, they are using the space, but they are not using it economically. One of the tricks used by people who design malls is to provide few places where people feel comfortable sitting for long without buying something.

Synoikismos also connotes the significance of peoples' shared experience. For the Greeks, the *agora* was a place that came out of the problem of having to be with people unlike oneself, a place for confronting differences. The *agora* was a center for talk, discussion, and shopping. (The market function was intermittent—the markets had closed by nine in the morning—but the *agoras* were used all day). To put it another way, the center is turf that people have fought for and in some way suffered for. It develops the sense of belonging that Londoners had after World War II. It was turf that mattered because something important had been lived there. To have a meaningful city center, something has to happen in it politically. The Greeks discovered this principle, and it is very simple and profound.

In the modern world we fear to use public space as the realm in which we learn to reconcile difference—or at least learn to coexist with it. One reflex action is to simulate past models of what public space *looked* like. People will say, "Let's do a Williamsburg. That's a time-tested mor-phology, right?" The plan of Williamsburg, Virginia, came out of the need to establish a colony in the midst of an alien and very threatening wilderness. The play of right angles in its spaces expressed a protective function. People created a certain kind of a center because they were in a hostile place. We can make modern cities look like old places, but we can-not recreate the social and economic circumstances that generated those models, even if we wanted to.

When we borrow only the look of history, we end up with Disney World as public space. It is no accident that Disney World is the most apparently successful, if simulated, public space created in the 1970s in America. It is a place where nothing painful happens, a place that com-pletely depoliticizes the experience of being in a public place.

Privatizing and Policing the Places We Meet

Another way Americans attempt to avoid the collision of differentness is through the privatization of public space. If you want to assemble the places people work, live, and attend school so that, for instance, workers can have onsite daycare for their children, you go outside the city, find a piece of land, and build a campus—some housing, a school, medical facili-ties, and a factory. That's not public, it's a company town. It doesn't represent any notion of shared experience and it doesn't confront the fact of difference. To be successful, some aspect of this place must be disso-nant; it must require people to say, "This is one way to live, but that is another." Then you have created a public realm. We're in trouble in urban studies because we cannot honestly think of forms of the public realm that are appropriate to the pains of our society.

Three specific problems emerge that must be considered if we are to work through the role of "the public" in public space. The first, and most elemental, is how to use public space so that people who are unlike get to talk to one another. In other words, how do we use public space as a forum for discourse? In thinking about the city as a place where people have to learn to talk to others, what might otherwise seem the minutiae of planning or design turn out to be incredibly important, like whether a park bench faces another park bench or simply the passing stream of traffic. Policing—the regulation of the public realm—is implicated, too. Police today—and this is not their fault—are trained to think they've got someone crazy on their hands if they get up and start speaking to a crowd of people. You can't have a public realm—you can't have *synoikismos*—if people don't exchange with one another, and the element of exchange is talk.

The second issue is the geography of justice, that is, how we study the ecology of the city in terms of questions of justice. David Harvey, in his wonderful book, *Social Justice and the City* (Johns Hopkins University Press, 1973), puts forward the notion that the seams of cities, where areas join, is where all the public action is. *Synoikismos* should happen where unlikes join. But we have devised a whole civil-engineering language for sealing off the social edges of cities, because we are afraid of what might happen at those seams. We are used to thinking that the best way to deal with a "potentially explosive" situation is to segregate the possible combatants by fast-moving traffic. That depoliticizes the city, and everybody loses because it means that people with differences don't interact. We need a way to reconceive the city so that we can locate the geography of justice and injustice. How about capitalizing on *synoikismos* by manipulating the edges where poor and rich people are, where business and residence meet? How about finding ways of making the city what it actually is, a place where those who are unlike find some sense of mattering to each other?

Civic Ethics

The third bedeviling issue—the one that is most philosophical and therefore the one that is most practical—is how space can serve the community's moral purposes. Space is subject to the moral constraints of community. The problem is, we do not know how to translate the ways in which we think ethically into any kind of physical equivalents. An exam-

The transparent envelope wrapping the Queensborough Public Library reveals the activities within, inviting the city's diverse ethnic population—including patrons of the farmers' market across the street—to come in and give it a try.

ple is the question of drugs, which is a problem with a spatial dimension in cities. Street-drug dealers essentially require a territory that only they occupy. In New York City, they once colonized parks, such as Union Square or Washington Square, gradually driving other people out. On a purely practical level, we need to find a way to restore such homogenized spaces to their role as places that serve many different kinds of people.

I, who was born left-wing and will die left-wing, have become a proponent of police harassment. I now understand the logic of daily arrests. The dealer who is arrested, even if he is out on the street the next day, has not been doing business for eight hours, and eventually the people who buy from him may move on as they find their supplies disrupted.

How we create spaces that operate morally (that is, serve diverse populations) is a physical-design question as well. Union Square was a happy haven for dealers of cocaine for so long because it had been designed as, essentially, a podium, with its ground plane raised more than three and a half feet above the surrounding streets. It was also ringed with a nice fringe of boxwood. Both elements obscured surveillance from the outside, so the dealers transacted business with little fear of passersby or police. In redesigning the park, the city cut the box hedges down, ripped out trees, and cut into the podium. They opened it up so that now the sightline from any part of the park is clear across. That gave old people, of whom there are many in that area of the city, the confidence that they could use the park without subjecting themselves to the dealers.

Now that is a kind of terrible example of the way in which moral values can be enacted through design. You create visibility so that you can displace the population that had colonized the space. A more positive way of looking at this issue is to consider, for instance, how we can keep poor people, but also lower-middle-class people and middle-class people, in and near centers of cities that are growing or becoming more prosperous. Gentrification tends to target people who have been around for a long time, who have toughed out the hard times and kept neighborhoods alive when others fled. Suddenly all this cash comes in—the dollar amounts look incredible—and the neighborhood falls apart or becomes a wealthier monoculture. If cities are to be civic or civil places, don't we owe it to ourselves to create a means akin to moral zoning to protect those most vulnerable, those who have given of themselves to keep the city going through the bad times?

If cities are to be anything more than ephemeral constructs of economic transaction, people must feel that something really important—something absolutely critical to their lives—happens because they are in a certain place. This subjects a host of political, economic, and zoning questions to an examination that is not moralizing, but moral. Americans are not comfortable conflating the political and moral in this way. It's not surprising, therefore, that so much of America is placeless. But much of what urbanists do today is to try to get a sense of what it means to create a public realm that is truly public—neither a simulation of a historical model, nor the withdrawal implied by the little community where everything is controlled, the campus where everything is done in private. What we should strive for is public work done in cities, and in public.

Richard Sennett is a professor of sociology and chair of The Cities Programme at the London School of Economics. He is also author of numerous books, including *Flesh and Stone: The Body and the City in Western Civilization*.

Public Places
Selected Projects

1

Parks

The ingredients of urban parks nowa-days go far beyond trees and grass. The 19th-century idea of a park as a place of passive recreation has given way to a diversity of purposes. Active sports take on ever-more diverse forms, but parks are also gathering places, whether for informal family picnics or huge summer music and arts festivals.

The mist from a fountain envelops a lone stroller at Harvard University, but the water seeping amidst the rocks might also draw a small child's touch.

Some parks remain quiet refuges, but a waterfront park will draw a crowd on a balmy day if careful design offers lots to see and good places to perch, as does the promenade that lines a cleaned-up industrial canal in Milwaukee.

Bryant Park has always been an oasis of green in the stone canyons of mid-town Manhattan. Frequent public events, and a design that discourages drug dealers through more open sight-lines, has made the restored park more popular than ever.

Giant spherical "beach pebbles" and a miniature balance bar evoke Santa Monica's "muscle beach" past in an ocean-shore play area for children. The adult version, spruced up, remains a beachside hot spot.

2

3

4

1   Photo: © Peter Aaron/Esto

Public Buildings

Design can help communities express their unique character or it can symbolize widely held values. A public building need not be imposing or grand, but there is a place for dignity and civic aspiration.

Against the razzmatazz of the Las Vegas Strip, for example, a single monumental column, holding up a light-filtering canopy, asserts the dignity of the federal courts.

The Bainbridge Island City Hall finds inspiration in local rural building forms, like the cedar-sided barns that have long defined this small island's rural character. Large areas of glass and high windows over a lofty entrance

space create bright, inviting places for gathering within. It conveys in every detail a message that the government exists to serve citizens.

Important large public buildings can be imposing, but they can also become landmarks, places that feel like emblems of their cities. This is the case with the Phoenix Federal Courthouse, where a high, glass-enclosed space filters the strong desert sunlight into a grand, shadow-dappled public lobby. Its serenity recognizes that the stress of encountering the justice system— as witness, plaintiff, juror, judge, staff-member, or interested observer— requires the provision of a place of calm and reassurance.

1
Lloyd D. George United States Courthouse, Las Vegas, Nevada; Cannon Dworsky/HCA with Langdon Wilson, architects

2
Bainbridge Island City Hall, Bainbridge Island, Washington; Miller/Hull Partnership, architect

3
Sandra Day O'Connor United States Courthouse, Phoenix, Arizona; Richard Meier & Partners, architect

2

3   Photo: © Scott Frances/Esto

Libraries

Libraries, especially in suburban communities are much more than repositories of books. They convey a sense of uniqueness and community solidarity that some very new places otherwise don't have. They act as on-line conduits to the outside world for those who can't get around much and can't afford computers. Their meeting rooms, often open long after hours, make them real community builders.

Amidst the cacophony of New York City's borough of Queens, the Polshek Partnership installed a glass-clad oasis—a dignified yet contemporary image for a library. It gently rounds the acute-angled corner to create a welcoming entrance and a sunny breathing space on the crowded streets.

The Allston Branch Library fits into its residential neighborhood by breaking its mass into handsome, welcoming components. It is undoubtedly a public, not a residential building but defers to the fine grain of its surroundings through an appealingly variegated, even sensual use of wood and stone shingles.

The exposed steel frame of the Philmon Library, in Atlanta, is both inexpensive and visually intriguing, while the richly sculpted space and playful rhythm of windows define appealing reading places.

1
Queensborough Public Library, Flushing, New York; The Polshek Partnership, architect

2
Allston Branch of the Boston Public Library; Machado and Silvetti Associates, architect

3
Lee G. Philmon Public Library, Riverdale, Georgia; Scogin Elam and Bray, architect

2

3

1

Memorials

In recent years Americans have redis-
covered a need to commemorate key
events and community values.
Memorials are among the most difficult
structures to design. But some truly
moving evocations of grief, hope, and
unity of national purpose have come out
of what can be protracted periods of
controversy during design.

In Boston, for example, gently lit
obelisks along a busy boulevard insis-
tently remind passersby of the human
cost of the Holocaust. Text incised on
the obelisks offers solace to those who
approach on foot.

A metal-lattice fence signals a garden
devoted to the struggle to win women
the right to vote. To express both the
local and national nature of this com-
memoration, horizontal metal ribbons
interweave a timeline and the lives of
Minnesota suffragettes. Stools at either
end of the fence display explanatory
plaques.

Letters from lost sailors have been
engraved on bronze sheets at the
Norfolk Armed Forces Memorial. But
the weighty material draws the attention of visitors because it has been
shaped like sheets of paper, which
appear to have wafted onto the plaza by
the breeze.

1
New England Holocaust
Memorial, Boston; Stanley
Saitowitz Office, architect

2
Minnesota Woman
Suffrage Memorial, St.
Paul; Loom, architect

3
Norfolk Armed Forces
Memorial, Norfolk,
Virginia; James Cutler,
architect

2

3

Great Streets

Allan Jacobs

In the United States, some 25 to 35 percent of a city's developed land is likely to be in public rights-of-way: streets. The percentages may vary in the older cities of Europe and Asia, but the amount of space devoted to streets is always significant. Streets are almost always owned by the public and intended for public use. When we speak of the "public realm," we are speaking in large measure of streets.

So when we look closer at cities we think of as great we usually find streets that are great. Bologna, Italy, is memorable for its gorgeously arcaded streets. Can we even remember what its buildings look like? It's hard to think of Paris without its grand boulevards carved out of the medieval city in the 19th century. The buildings that line these streets may be elegant and superficially different from each other, but the buildings are not the point. The streets are full of traffic and bustling passersby, strolling couples and window shoppers, all watched over by patrons tarrying at café tables.

Some streets are better to be on; they are better for doing what you came to do. In the Boulevard Saint-Michel in Paris, stores, book tables, and cafés spill out of similarly sized buildings, which are covered in dancing light. It's a much more pleasant street than Market Street in San Francisco, which is somehow uncomfortable, in places shabby, and without much grace whether one walks or drives. Buildings and stores line one side of Princess Street in Edinburgh. They look across to a park and

Lined with Chicago's great department stores and spectacular movie palaces, State Street has been among America's great commercial avenues. With the closing of the movie houses and the decline in downtown department-store shopping over two decades, the street seemed to have fallen on permanent hard times. After a concerted effort to lure a diversity of shopping and other commercial ventures, augmented by an energizing redesign of the sidewalks, lighting, and other street "furniture," the street has staged an impressive comeback.

to the old city and castle on the hill beyond. It is more compelling than Regent Street in London, regardless of the latter's unified architectural expression and dramatic crescent at Piccadilly Circus. Both were consciously intended to be great streets. On the other hand, Roslyn Place in Pittsburgh, a short cul-de-sac with large trees and red brick houses, pretends not at all to specialness, but its closeness is inviting and it is better to walk down and certainly better to live along than are countless suburban residential streets the world over.

The Uses of the Street

You go back to some streets more often than to others, and not just because one is more convenient or has along it places you need to visit more often. A street can unlock memories or offer expectations of something pleasant to be seen. On some streets you are more likely to meet someone you know or someone new. The street is movement, especially of people. It is an ever-changing tableau of tiny vignettes: of fleeting forms, faces, postures, dress. You stop to watch. They pass. They look you over—or they don't, absorbed in their own thoughts or conversations. You may speak to no one, yet find yourself comforted by other people's presence.

Many streets are places to do business, but some transcend their reason for being. They are public showcases, meant to exhibit what society has to offer, and to entice. The entrepreneur offers the goods, displays them to the street, indeed pushes them as far into the street as is allowed. The looker sees, compares, fingers, discusses a possible purchase with a companion, and ultimately decides to enter the store or stall, and crosses the threshold from the protection and anonymity of the public realm into the private place of exchange.

The street is also a political space. Main Street may offer a setting for a Fourth of July parade one day and an antinuclear march the next. The street is as important in playing out people's most cherished ideals as it is for any of its everyday uses. Even in the age of email politics, we still turn out on the street to make our views heard.

People understand that streets are more than a means for movement and access—that they have symbolic, ceremonial, social, and political roles to play. Citizens often object to high-volumes of fast traffic on their streets, but they will commonly tax themselves to make them special, "great" places. In 1967, San Franciscans spent millions to turn Market Street into a great street, designed specially to accommodate parades. More than two decades later, they traded in the looming elevated structure of the earthquake-damaged Embarcadero Freeway for a handsomely designed avenue. Chicago, Denver, Minneapolis, Santa Cruz, Sacramento, Toledo, and Iowa City are but a few of hundreds of large and small cities that have recently made street design more important.

What Makes a Street Great?

A great street should help make community. It should help people to act and interact to achieve in concert what they might not achieve alone. Accordingly, better streets are accessible to all, easy to find, and easy to get to. There you want to see other people, all kinds of people, whatever their age, color, or class, and feel comfortable meeting them. Consider Curitiba, in Brazil, where, for more than 15 years, people have been laying a long, long strip of paper down the main street every Saturday morning. Wooden sticks, staked every meter or so, hold the paper in place. Parents and friends bring children who, offered brushes and paint, make pictures on the hundreds of white surfaces. It's a scene of public display and camaraderie, of easy conversation. Social or economic status is neither an impediment nor an advantage to joining in. Desire is the only prerequisite.

Streets come alive when people who occupy adjacent buildings add something to the mix. Signs, awnings, flowers, a stoop for sitting—all are contributions that elicit a response, or even a dialog from passersby.

The pattern of streets, blocks, and buildings gives character to streets. Manhattan's wide north-south avenues, lined with tall buildings and street-level stores, contrast with the quiet, much-narrower, brown-stone-lined side streets. A city made of one or the other would be dull; together they are rich. The blocks William Penn laid out in 17th-century Philadelphia are made more beautiful, many would argue, with the contrast offered by the many tiny alleys with equally tiny houses burrowed through them by early American speculators.

There is magic to great streets. The best are as joyful as they are utilitarian. They are symbols of a community and its history; they represent a public memory. They are places for escape and for romance, places to act and to dream.

Allan Jacobs, an architect and city planner, has been planning director in San Francisco and has worked in Pittsburgh, Boston, and Calcutta. Author of four books, he has consulted the world over, most happily in Curitiba, Brazil. He taught urban design at the University of California, Berkeley, for over 20 years.

Streets
Selected Projects

1

No one would mistake America's ubiquitous freeways and commercial strips for the boulevards of Paris, but designers are finding new means of breathing life into these vast landscapes of concrete.

Spaced along the broad avenues and freeway ramps that lead to the Los Angeles International airport, brightly lit pylons create a pleasurable entry sequence.

State Street, in Chicago, has been rescued from an ill-fated pedestrian scheme with new attention to sidewalks, wastebaskets, and street trees.

Kettner Row, a residential project in San Diego, enlivens its street with ground-level units that can be used for living or a home-based business.

Where once the din of an elevated highway drove people away from San Francisco's waterfront, a crescent-shaped urban plaza now makes a grand culmination to Market Street and an entrance to the historic ferry terminal. Designers collaborated with the local port agency, the transportation department, and the transit agency to extend an appealing boulevard along the route of the demolished freeway. It coordinates traffic lanes and new trolley tracks with handsomely designed sidewalks, bike lanes, and planting. Opening the old Embarcadero to the harbor has spurred new development along its length.

1
Approach to Los Angeles International Airport; Ted Tokio Tanaka architects with Moody Ravitz Hollingsworth Lighting Design, artist Paul Tzanetopoulos, and the Lighting Design Alliance

2
State Street Renovation Project, Chicago; Skidmore Owings & Merrill, architect

3
Kettner Row, San Diego; Jonathan Segal, architect, developer

4 / 5
Mid-Embarcadero Open Space and Transportation Project, San Francisco; Roma Design Group, architect

2

3

4

5

69

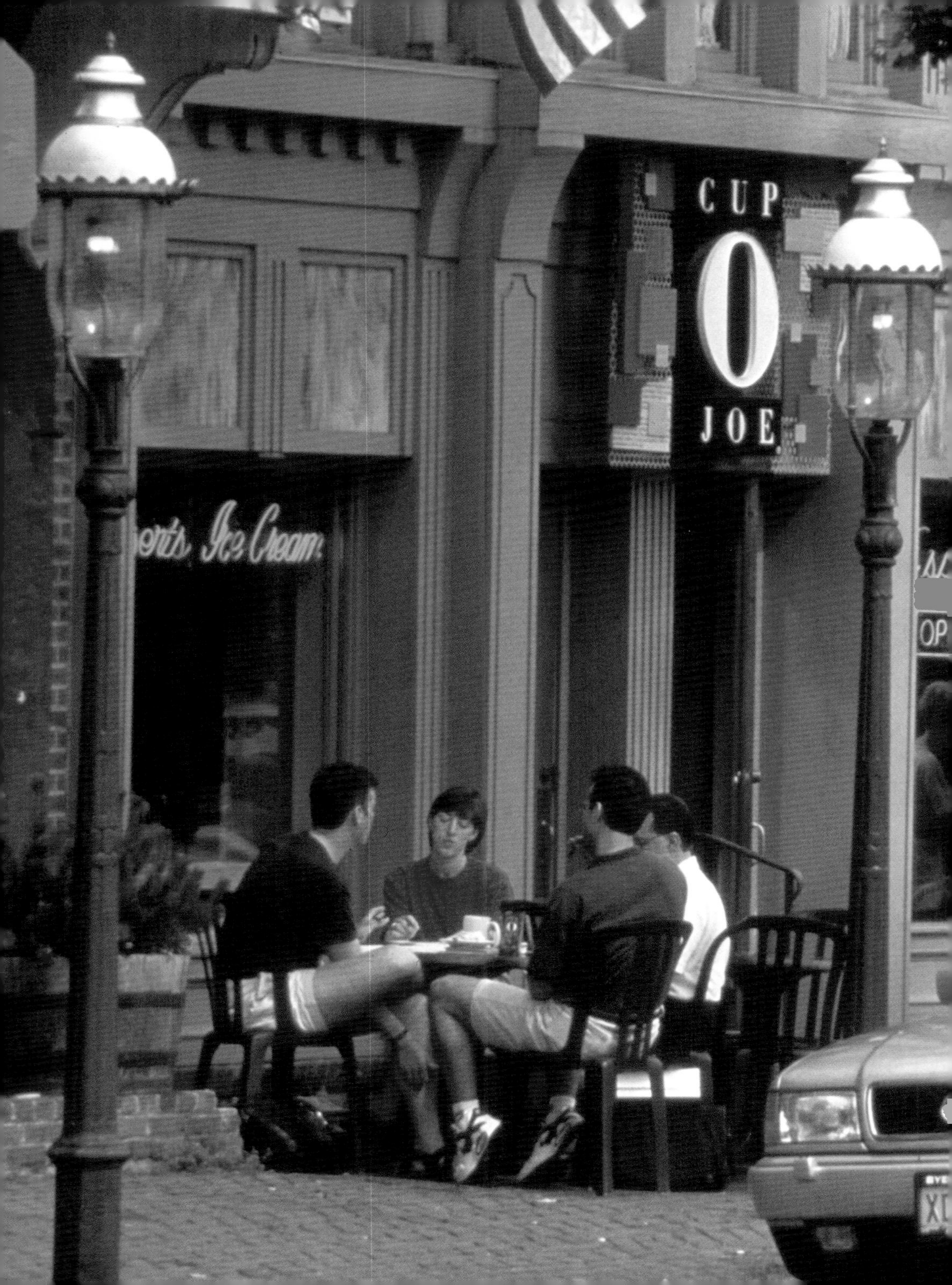
CUP
O
JOE.
Ice Cream

Elements of Success in Downtown Revitalization

Donovan D. Rypkema

Over the last 15 years hundreds of downtowns in America have experienced a remarkable comeback. In towns and cities of every size, in every part of the country, city centers that were written off as nearly dead are today thriving centers of living, working, shopping, and playing. It would be difficult, however, to identify an example of sustained success in downtown revitalization that was a spontaneous result of the marketplace acting on its own. Invariably, local actions were undertaken that first recognized the inherent importance of the downtown to the city, and, second, took steps to reverse decline that may have gone unchecked for decades.

While the approach to downtown revitalization varies from community to community, there does seem to be a set of common denominators—elements of success in downtown revitalization—that emerges. While not every revitalization success story includes every element, the vast majority of sustained successes includes the vast majority of these elements.

The sight of cafes spilling onto a street of handsomely restored buildings was once a rarity, but is now increasingly common and popular, thanks to the long-term efforts of local activists and the historic-preservation community. German Village, in Columbus, Ohio, is one of the oldest and most successful neighborhood preservation efforts.

Leadership and Government

Someone steps forward and says, "Downtown is important. The current condition of our downtown is unacceptable, and we need to do something about it." Sometimes that initial leadership comes from an elected official—the mayor or a council member—but frequently it comes from the business community. A banker might see a declining value in the portfolio of downtown real estate and in business loans. A chamber of commerce president could recognize the adverse impact that downtown's deteriorating state has on industrial recruitment efforts. A mayor might equate the health of the downtown with the image of the city overall. But in nearly every instance the memory of the vibrant, active downtown that once was triggers a consensus that the center city's current condition is unacceptable.

Whether or not a public official provided the initial leadership, active support from and participation by City Hall is a central component of nearly all successful downtown revitalization stories. Public-sector investment, particularly in infrastructure and amenities, plays an important role in a downtown revitalization effort. However, there is often the temptation to do too much—to make downtown "cute" rather than making improvements that are functional and appropriate for the context, scale, and history of the downtown. Downtown leaders too often convince themselves that physical improvements—the bigger the better—are the answer to declining downtowns. Numerous cities have built new brick walkways, added street trees, benches, decorative streetlights, and parking garages, and made grants for façade restorations, and yet still suffer from vacant buildings and pedestrian-free sidewalks. Physical improvements are a piece of a comprehensive approach to downtown revitalization, not the total solution.

The Who and How of Reinvestment

Most downtown-revitalization strategies include a range of financial incentives that encourage reinvestment within a carefully defined area. The particular incentives available vary from place to place and are often dependent on enabling statutes in state law. Any of the following are beneficial (and there are numerous others) if targeted as part of a strategy connected to the city's unique circumstances: tax-increment financing, business-improvement districts, tax abatements, land write-downs, low-interest loans, fee waivers, and public occupancy (of an office building, say, to show commitment and spur other commitment).

The phrase "public-private partnership" is widely used to describe the means by which downtown revitalization is organized. In reality, however, an independent nonprofit organization usually manages revitalization efforts. This entity serves as the vehicle through which the public and private sectors, as well as the nonprofit community, participate in charting a new direction for downtown. If a city attempts to act alone in revitalization, it is seen as "just another government program." If the business community approaches downtown revitalization as the sole participant, the public will perceive a motivation that is self-serving at best. A nonprofit organization will rarely have the financial means or the political muscle to undertake the effort single-handedly. But the mutual efforts of the three sectors have proven to be dependably successful.

Twenty years ago some experts believed that downtown could cede its old role as a central business district and survive as the city's government and financial center. Cities that pursued that strategy ended up with downtowns virtually vacant 16 hours a day. Revitalization advocates in more successful cities have promoted a multifunctional downtown of great diversity. Downtown should be a center for business, government, arts and culture, medicine, and education. It should be a place where people live and shop and explore their various heritages, a place that attracts tourists and locals, convention-goers, special-events attendees, and sports fans. Diversity does not just make downtown fun and attractive, it generates the small firms that feed the big firms and creates a location that can support specialized businesses that serve the entire metro region.

Buildings and People

The relative importance of restoring and adapting treasured older buildings varies from city to city according to the wealth of historic structures that exist. Any expert would be hard pressed, however, to identify a single example of sustained success in downtown revitalization where the preservation and re-use of the city's unique built environment was not a key component of the overall strategy. It is a community's historic buildings that provide, more than anything else, a sense of differentiation, a sense of place, and constitute the physical manifestation of a city's unique history and character.

As multifunctionality is a component of most successfully revitalized downtowns, so too is mixing uses within buildings and projects. Adding residential and entertainment uses to the usual downtown blend of office and commercial uses extends the hours that both the building and the downtown are lively, provides a synergy between uses and users, yields counter-cyclical use of parking, and even mitigates the natural ups and downs in the real-estate market by diversifying risk. The value of mixed use is true both for larger new projects and the adaptive re-use of older "white-elephant" structures. To allow, for example, live/work lofts or permit residential use next to commercial use may require changes in both zoning ordinances and building codes.

Dozens of measurements can be used to judge the health of a downtown, but the answer to one question alone tends to reliably predict success: are there people on the street? If the answer is "yes," the downtown will prove to be vital by most other measures; if the answer is "no," it will not. While successful downtowns are multifunctional with each component adding value to the whole, the presence of people tends to attract more people. Four activities add great numbers of people to the street: retailing, food and beverage venues, entertainment, and housing. Successful downtowns re-establish the pedestrian orientation that cities had early in the 20th century. Automobiles are accommodated—for both circulation and parking—but no longer at the expense of people on foot.

A Vision That Creates a Sense of Place

While officials understandably want to see dramatic success before the next election, most downtown revitalization success stories are built one business, one building, one block at a time. There is no "quick fix." Success comes gradually over a period of years. As there is no "quick fix," neither is there a single "big fix." Megaproject advocates will claim, "It was our stadium/convention center/aquarium/children's museum/hotel/sports arena/festival marketplace/et cetera that spurred the rebirth of our downtown." But such is almost never actually the case. Revitalized city centers may include major projects, but lasting success comes out of multiple catalysts for change, beginning with small-scale efforts (like the rehabilitation of historic structures by students or artists) that take place over time.

In most instances an early step in the revitalization process is the establishment of a "vision" for the downtown. It may be little more than a wish list drawn up by a downtown committee. An extended and highly participatory process involving the entire community is a more ambitious process that will not only identify a host of ideas, but also often produce a kind of consensus that will help ideas move forward. However it is done, establishing a framework that identifies goals and priorities for the revitalization process is common to most downtown success stories.

Cities with healthy and diverse museums, galleries, theaters, performance spaces, studios, public art, and festivals involve more of their own people and attract more visitors. Arts and cultural activities bring more people out over longer hours, with much more economic, racial, educational, and age diversity than any "big fix" megaprojects, such as convention centers and sports stadiums. City leaders too often regard arts and culture as nice but not critical to economic rejuvenation. In fact, cities are proving that the arts are a key component of revitalization. Because many arts activities—particularly in the early and experimental stages—rely on relatively low-cost space, downtown buildings where the rent levels are appreciably lower than in the office park or the shopping center often serve as arts incubators. This adds vibrancy to downtown and catalyzes growth in surrounding areas.

Successful downtowns have figured out that their revitalization strategy should not make them *like* another city (or, worse yet, like a shopping center). Instead they capitalize on what makes them unique, differentiating themselves from anywhere else. They must first identify the distinctive elements of the local built and natural environments, including cultural, environmental, and economic attributes, then protect and enhance them.

In successful revitalization efforts there is a sense of public ownership that extends far beyond those who hold deeds to land. Downtown becomes the place identified with the entire city, a place with which citizens feel solidarity, the place that sums up all the diverse metropolitan communities—city and suburb alike. Festivals, celebrations, and even protests organized in and for the downtown are vital elements in creating this sense of ownership. The idea that "this is *my* downtown" must be broadly felt within the community to develop the political and public support necessary for what is inherently an ongoing and possibly costly process.

Downtown advocates and particularly elected officials don't want failures in their revitalization efforts. But a once-promising flop is evidence that someone had confidence—in short it's evidence that revitalization has begun. Communities that don't experience at least a few failures during the revitalization process are probably taking too few risks and may find their improvement efforts losing momentum.

The cobbled side street lined by row houses, with a café or a gallery; the once-neglected alleyway filling with new, one-of-a-kind boutiques—these are the special places that lure people to revitalizing downtowns and that cannot be duplicated by chain stores in a mall. Part of keeping the sense of discovery alive is having cleanliness without sterility, and offering a sense of safety without losing a sense of adventure.

Donovan D. Rypkema is principal of Place Economics, a Washington-based economic development consulting firm.

Downtown Revitalization
Selected Projects

1

Big and small strategies by public agencies and private enterprises animate once-struggling downtowns. To diversify beyond office towers and parking lots, cities have added amenities to draw in residents and attractions to create a destination appealing regionally, nationally, and even internationally.

At Yerba Buena Gardens, in San Francisco, a park was placed on the roof of a sunken convention center. Two museums and a performing arts center surround the park and have drawn commercial development and housing, and attracted additional cultural institutions.

As part of a long-time series of downtown enhancements, Providence uncovered a paved-over part of the Providence River and installed in its place the Waterplace Park and Riverwalk, promenades, bridges, and plazas inspired by Venice. Its focal point is the aptly named WaterFire installation.

South Beach, in Miami, started small, with the efforts of Art Deco building aficionados to breathe new life into a moribund neighborhood. The pace of building restoration and new construction has skyrocketed in recent years. A center of fashion, retail, and media, it is now one of the liveliest and most vital downtowns in America.

1/ 2
Yerba Buena Gardens;
San Francisco; MGA
Partners, architect

3
Waterplace Park and
Riverwalk, Providence,
Rhode Island; William
Warner, architect

4
Ocean Drive in South
Beach, Miami

2

3

4

Civil Engineering for Cities

James S. Russell

On the Upper West Side of Manhattan, as in so many other places, a highway cuts off access between the city and the river. But unlike the massive concrete conduits filled with hordes of vehicles found in so many other places, the six lanes of the Henry Hudson Parkway exist in a uniquely benign relationship to the city and the river. The parkway runs through Riverside Park, and a combination of stone-faced walls, handsome metal decorative fences, and beautiful arched bridges dampen the noise and give frequent inviting access to the river. Underneath the park runs a two-track rail line. The promenade of Riverside Drive forms the park's inland edge, swooping in its own counterpoint to the elegantly curved line of residential buildings along the drive.

Few people find a rail line and a freeway desirable neighbors, but if more places in America were as sensitively designed as this strip of land, they would be as sought after as Riverside Drive is today.

The planning and construction of every public work presents a community with an opportunity. More cities are recognizing that ordinary structures like roads, train stations, airports, parking structures, bus stations, power-generating plants, and telecommunications towers, can lend a place grace and identity. Until recent decades, public works were deemed worthy of the highest level of design attention. Hoover Dam would not be one of Nevada's busiest tourist attractions today if it had not been so exquisitely fitted into its canyon site. Coastal communities

The International Terminal at San Francisco International Airport must move passengers not only on and off planes but in and out of autos, buses, a rapid-transit line, and a light rail line. A lofty ticketing hall delicately diffuses sunlight through trusses shaped like boat hulls, wrapped with light-transmitting fabric. But the hall's architecture aids wayfinding, easing what for many people is a stressful, confusing, and demeaning experience.

cherish their prosaic lighthouses because the evocative quality of their design has lived long beyond their functional utility. Consider the visitor who arrives at an airport that is spacious, well-maintained, and light-filled. It shows you the way by the clarity of its layout, and reunites you with your luggage minutes after your arrival. If you are considering moving your family or locating a business in a city with such an airport, it inspires confidence.

Added Value Infrastructure

While airport operators now recognize the importance of a welcoming facility, the similar potential in other kinds of public works also deserves recognition. A bridge can almost single-handedly define the identity of a city, as the Golden Gate Bridge does for San Francisco. An interstate highway can slice a city in two, or a park can be created over the freeway, as Seattle did, to knit neighborhoods together and make a popular gathering spot at the same time. A recycling center may seem just another undesirable building. But with some careful attention from artists and designers, it can become—as it has in Phoenix—a visitor magnet and an educational boon.

The value of a well-designed, well-loved infrastructure project is nearly incalculable, but the initial costs are, unfortunately, all too real to the officials who must ask communities to pay for them. Officials sometimes must overcome the limitations of state and federal grantmaking rules, which too often view making public works publicly pleasing as a frill. On the federal level, at least, this attitude has begun to change. It is now permissible to use federal transportation funding for a variety of enhancements, ranging from creating bicycle paths to restoring historic transportation structures. Sometimes the ratio of design attention to impact is impressive. In Los Angeles, for example, the Metro Rapid express busses have been highly successful in part because the appealing and highly recognizable graphics and bus-shelter designs constantly remind traffic-jammed drivers that they have an option.

Various funding exists to lessen local problems associated with the construction or expansion of critical infrastructure projects. Here the inventiveness of the designer can often reconcile the project's needs with the concerns of neighbors. The artful, concrete-framed, shrubbery-filled contours that wrap the West Point Sewage Treatment plant in Seattle not only screen the plant, but also have turned this prominent spot into an attraction for beach strollers and hikers. What about a parking structure and bus station in the middle of downtown? The Leamington Municipal Transit Hub in Minneapolis is a stylish, abstract composition that makes even parked cars part of the artwork.

Integrating and Collaborating

The Leamington hub is an example of another emerging infrastructure trend, combining what were once regarded as unrelated facilities. The idea is not new: 19th-century water reservoirs were frequently artfully incorporated into parks. Today, bikeways link to bus-transit interchanges, and rail-transit systems are increasingly extended to airports, where a number of cities plan links to long distance trains. Such multi-modal interchanges can also become commercial hubs.

Engineers usually lead infrastructure projects, but the most community-oriented works usually result from the collaboration of engineers with other design professionals. The Phoenix recycling project was designed with an artist, the Seattle sewage project with a landscape architect. Such projects work best when there is a genuine desire to collaborate, an understanding of respective roles, and a willingness to work with the community to realize its desires.

Infrastructure projects, perhaps uniquely, permit engineering to come forward as a language of aesthetic expressiveness. Each element of a road bridge—girders, abutments, columns, and decks—can be taken as an opportunity to create a project that recognizes topography, that fits into a built-up community, or that celebrates the spanning of a river. The design of the Bay Area Rapid Transit System in the San

Francisco Bay Area and the Metro transit system in Washington, D.C., are both elegant and highly functional examples of engineering and architecture operating almost seamlessly together. While communities all over America battle unsightly cellphone towers and radio antennae, many European cities have amalgamated these functions into telecommunications towers, which have often been created as award-winning essays in elegant engineering.

Infrastructure is so ubiquitous that opportunities are easily overlooked. A storm-water retention pond can be a pit lined by plastic sheeting surrounded by a few straggly grasses or, with a little greater attention, it can be a shrub-and-tree lined oasis for passersby and shelter for a seasonally changing panorama of wildlife.

Infrastructure
Selected Projects

1

Collaborations of artists, designers, and engineers are breathing life into the civil-engineering backbone of cities.

Landscaped, undulating contours transform a drainage channel into a place for people and wildlife in the Guadaloupe River Park. A small amphitheater serves double duty during severe storms, absorbing the river's overflow.

The services of an artist and architect turned a prosaic recycling center in Phoenix into a dramatic sculpture and a teaching tool, while one in semi-rural Vashon Island, Washington, makes the chore of sorting trash almost a pleasure.

The simple vault of a bus station roof is a welcoming symbol for Winston-Salem. Its openness also inspires a sense of security for patrons.

1
Guadaloupe River Park, San Jose, California; Hargreaves Associates, landscape architects

2
27th Avenue Solid Waste Management Facility, Phoenix, Arizona; Linnea Glatt, Michael Singer, artists, with Sterling McMurrin, architect, and Black & Veatch, engineers

2

3

4

5

3
Transportation Center,
Winston-Salem, North
Carolina; Walter Robbs
Callahan & Pierce,
architect

4
Vashon Island Transfer
and Recycling Center,
Vashon Island,
Washington; Miller/Hull
Partnership, architect

5
International Terminal,
San Francisco
International Airport.
Skidmore, Owings &
Merrill with Campo &
Maru and Michael Willis
& Associates, architects

Making a Place for Housing

James S. Russell

There are few communities that could not use more affordable housing. In some, housing the needy and even the middle class is a chronic struggle. Communities on their own cannot solve housing problems, but many are finding that they can take a tactical and strategic role to both provide more housing and to use the development of housing as a catalyst to growth and revitalization.

Housing growth often leads commercial and job growth; indeed it can initiate it. The inner-city revival evident in so many cities began with artists, students, and gays who remodeled deteriorated houses and transformed abandoned industrial lofts for live/work studios. Such residential gentrification draws neighborhood commercial development, then spurs downtown revival as white-collar businesses decide to locate near the most creative and highly motivated workforce.

So if a community wants jobs or growth, it wants first to become an appealing place to live. The housing-first growth formula works best when affluent people choose a given neighborhood, but mixed-income housing growth can also draw jobs because companies increasingly seek to locate in places where positions at every level can readily be filled. Cities can aid revitalization or growth by targeting grants or tax advantages in those areas with the greatest potential, by strategically improving services and infrastructure, and by encouraging neighborhood-commercial businesses like grocery stores, drug stores, laundries, and hardware stores to locate in targeted areas. In addition, a

It may share its busy commercial street frontage with car washes and convenience stores, but Pensione Esperanza holds its own on the strip with a glassy corner entrance that is both sculptural and lighthearted. (A neon sign reminds passersby that the site was once a used-car lot.) The project serves one of San Jose's neediest populations by providing 110 single-occupancy rooms, augmented by on-site social services, a library, community kitchen, and other amenities.

89

city can often encourage private housing development by purchasing land, rezoning, and providing improved infrastructure. Tax abatements or other aid may also be required in early stages.

Most housing aid comes from the federal government in the form of tax advantages offered to homebuyers. Government aid to families that cannot afford to own is far more limited and complex to secure, requiring communities to be highly inventive in the way they encourage "affordable" (below-market) or subsidized housing. A given development may use federal Section-8 vouchers, low-income-housing tax credits, and public-housing subsidies, often combined with similar state and local grant or tax-abatement programs.

For subsidized projects, communities today increasingly rely on locally based nonprofit developers or for-profit developers that make a specialty of such housing. The for-profits are especially useful to augment local community developers who may have insufficient expertise in the complexities of housing development.

High-quality design can reduce neighborhood resistance to subsidized tenants and improve the commitment of potential renters, who do not feel the "project" stigma. Some of the most successful housing mixes market-rate and subsidized tenants within the same development.

A design process that includes a great deal of neighborhood involvement usually smoothes the way to approval. New housing development can bring with it fears of gentrification, increased traffic, or, contrarily, fears that "government" housing might reduce property values. Housing in a traditionally troubled community might have to be developed hand-in-hand with a strategy to address problems in schools, public health, job training, and inadequate cultural and recreational activities. New housing can augment its value to the neighborhood by incorporating, for instance, a badly needed daycare facility, a recreational center, or—as in a recent project in Oakland, California—a farmers' market.

Housing design must often walk a fine line. Local activists may demand more from affordable projects than from market-rate ones; funders may expect low-income projects to cost less to build; managers may want more costly institutional-quality finishes because they have fewer maintenance resources. Though housing development is undeniably complex, its rewards are substantial, both to individuals, now well housed, and to the civic and economic life of the city.

Housing
Selected Projects

1

Inventive architects and sponsors have created housing below market rates of enormous appeal and inventiveness in spite of harrowing financial and bureaucratic barriers.

Side stair entrances lead to heat-beating porches for low-income housing in steamy Charleston. The Race Street Row Houses evoke in a contemporary way a type that has long characterized the city.

In San Diego, where housing costs are high, Mission Terrace offers an affordable alternative for workers in the many nearby hotels. The courtyarded structures step up the hill over a two-level parking structure.

Top-floor apartments, reached by an elevator and a zigzag walkway that shades the quiet play court, surmount townhouses in an income-assisted project in Santa Monica. Even though the project was built at high density, it generously houses families.

A group of local housing activists championed Langham Court, which affordably matched the quality of adjacent homes in its historic neighborhood, mixing incomes to maintain community and project stability. (There's no visible distinction between market-rate and subsidized units.)

Neighbors may "NIMBY" the idea of single-room occupancy housing, but the fresh, inventive design of Pensione Esperanza, sponsored by a local Catholic charity, won over skeptics.

2

3

4

5

Life at the Water's Edge

James S. Russell

Few people can resist the changing reflections at the water's edge or the sound of waves breaking on a bulkhead. That's why the Inner Harbor virtually defines Baltimore and Chicago would be unthinkable without Grant Park sprawling along the shores of Lake Michigan. But even cities without the maritime history of San Francisco or Norfolk are learning to make waterfronts a key aspect of their appeal and a magnet for residents and visitors alike. The presence or the view of water isn't enough, however. Waterfront design succeeds when it mingles with the very fabric of the city itself, bringing the smell, touch, and sound of water closer.

The form of Chicago's park dates from the 19th-century idea that parks were green, carefully ordered places for passive recreation. Thirty years ago, Baltimore pioneered the transformation from industrial waterfront to commercial center and visitor attraction. But these are hardly the only models cities can choose today. Indeed, officials must often be highly creative in the way they transform waterfronts, because acquiring the vast tracts that made both the Baltimore and Chicago projects possible can be difficult.

Other barriers must be overcome to use waterfronts effectively. There's always been lots of competition for urban waterfront space. Historically, shipping interests jostled with water-using industries, which got in the way of fishing fleets and ferries. It was often easiest to run rail lines or highways along river corridors and baysides, where they formed

What was once an intensely industrial riverfront is finding new life as loft buildings redevelop for residential and commercial uses. Milwaukee's RiverWalk offers a civic-scaled means to stroll and boat from one downtown destination to another along the cleaned-up river.

effective physical barriers to many public uses. And the need to undertake the costly cleanup of toxic residues can impede the conversion of former docklands or other waterfront industrial sites.

The enormous appeal of water very often overcomes the political and financial complexities. San Antonio remade itself through its Riverwalk. Pittsburgh and Cleveland are steadily reclaiming riversides that once teemed with pollutants, repairing their reputations for livability in the process. Mills that once spilled tannery waste and raw sewage into streams and canals have been transformed into chic loft residences facing water bodies now clean enough for swimming.

Part of the wonder of waterfronts is that success can be achieved through a diversity of means. But some broad principles have been shown to assure success.

Cities need not create pure passive parks nor cram waterfronts with amusements to succeed. Cleaned-up industries often make good neighbors of water-oriented recreational uses like marinas or boat-maintenance facilities. Wildlife may thrive even in an island of estuarine marshland adjacent to a busy shipping channel. Small beaches or lake-viewing docks can be erected at street ends. Powerboating, fishing, kayaking, bird-watching, swimming, and excursion-boat tours can all share the same stretch of waterfront, if the traffic (both landborne and waterborne) is orchestrated with sensitivity. Passersby are attracted to more activity and more diverse activity.

Communities should aspire to make a sense of place. A dusty parking lot and a cracked sidewalk on a crumbling bulkhead with a view to a murky, trash-strewn stream does not make a waterfront. Nearly every site has unique aspects that can be drawn out by sensitive design: an attractive grouping of wildlife-attracting native plants, an appealing confluence of landform and sea, even something unique in the light reflected off the water. Vistas to the open sea can be enhanced by height or enclosures that frame and focus the view. Consider also how the city is seen from the waterfront. The magic of Seattle's, San Francisco's, or New York's waterfront is enhanced by the towers that rise up from their edges.

Don't privatize the waterfront. Numerous commercial and private uses can share shorelines with the public. A waterside boulevard, board-walk, or promenade can serve diverse private uses along the waterfront without precluding public use. Too many cities reap only minor benefit from beachfronts walled-off by insensitively built condo towers, for example.

Recognize the dynamic nature of shore environments. Too many ocean-front communities have entirely lost their beaches by permitting construction that disregarded their ecology. Streams flood, tides flow in and out; erosion (often exacerbated by human activity) will change a lake-front's configuration. Floating docks, carefully placed log booms, and water-edge plantings—along with boat-speed restrictions—can reduce shore erosion.

What can be toughest about waterfront development is the expense. Piers, bulkheads, and beach restoration are costly. Cleaning polluted industrial sites is even more expensive, and relocating railroads or highways is often out of the question. But cities are finding lots of ways around these barriers. Many waterfront projects can be done incrementally. Exceedingly modest improvements—street-end parks, a bike path, a wildlife trail through a restored wetlands—can build a constituency for more ambitious redevelopment. San Francisco has taken down its much-reviled Embarcadero Freeway, replacing it with an appealing auto and transit boulevard and opening sparkling vistas to the bay. But Louisville slid its Waterfront Park gracefully under the massive bulk of Interstate 64 to reclaim its connection to the Ohio River.

The heritage of working waterfronts can often be incorporated as they get adapted for new uses. Industrial towns along Pennsylvania's Monongahela River are considering how to maintain the fascinating hulks of abandoned blast furnaces as they turn steelmaking sites into museums of industrial heritage in parks and commercial developments along the cleaned-up riverfront.

There are bureaucratic barriers that can be overcome when there is an early awareness of the complex requirements that must to be met. Besides the usual local codes, there are state coastal commissions and environmental boards. The U.S. Army Corps of Engineers has authority over navigable waters, which it shares with the Environmental Protection Agency when the alteration of wetlands is undertaken.

The fundamental appeal of water makes overcoming these barriers worthwhile. A stream, lake, or bay doesn't need much encouragement to work its magic.

Waterfronts
Selected Projects

1

As cities diversify from smokestack economies, they are transforming their industrial waterfronts, creating amenities that citizens (and quality of life–driven businesses) seek.

Richmond's Canal Walk turns a piece of industrial heritage—a barge canal—into an armature that unites the waterfront. The designers added special touches to break down barriers between adjacent neighborhoods and the river.

Art-festooned ramps, tucked into a 35-foot-wide strip along a busy highway, descend gently from downtown streets to the calm of the Allegheny River, in downtown Pittsburgh.

Former mills and warehouses now open onto a pedestrians-only riverside "street" in Milwaukee. And in Louisville, Hargreaves Associates found a way to turn a massive freeway into a sculptural element as it reclaimed the city's connection to the Ohio River.

1
Canal Walk, Richmond, Virginia; Wallace Roberts & Todd, landscape architect

2
Allegheny Riverfront Park, Pittsburgh, Pennsylvania; Michael Van Valkenburgh Associates, landscape architect; Ann Hamilton, Michael Mercil, artists

2

3

4

5

3
Milwaukee RiverWalk,
Milwaukee, Wisconsin;
Ken Kay Associates, urban
planner and landscape
architect

4 / 5
Louisville Waterfront Park,
Louisville, Kentucky;
Hargreaves Associates,
landscape architect

101

III

The Tools

Rules for Designing Cities

Alex Krieger

Comedian Woody Allen's claim that he is "two with nature" contains a useful insight into town design. The long-standing American yearning for the middle ground, in which the virtues of urbanity and nature are simultaneously enjoyed, may at last be proving itself a form of fool's gold, devaluing both country and city. Stated more positively, we may be at a point of understanding empirically what the early advocates of suburbia hypothesized. The idea of the suburb should not be about simulating city life amid nature. Rather, it is about maintaining proximity to both of the realms believed to be necessary for civilization to be sustained. At the center of suburban regions, cities might best nurture their own virtues and give up their longstanding attempt to emulate the arguably tenuous successes of suburbs. Following is an enumeration of several rules for designing cities.

The Beauty of Diversity

The spaces outside private property lines deserve as much attention as those inside. The work of urban designer Skidmore, Owings & Merrill on Chicago's State Street included sidewalk paving patterns, fenced planters, street trees, and subway-entrance canopies.

Aggregate things. The essential ingredient of a town is its density—not measured in square feet, but in the juxtaposition of artifice and activity. Engagement made possible by proximity is crucial, and much more difficult to sustain where things are spread out across great distances. You cannot have solitude *and* friendship *and* connection to the larger society without closeness.

Beware of homogeneity. We are often charmed by a wonderful diversity. Along a street, buildings need not look alike to be harmonious. Buildings, like citizens, warrant their personalities and idiosyncrasies as long as each behaves civilly toward the others. There is a kind of illusion of autonomy about suburban buildings spaced at intervals of half an acre or more; a civil presence seems less important when buildings are dotted over a vast landscape, and so it is less-often offered. It is much harder to be crass when you are arrayed cheek-by-jowl with your neighbor.

Believe in mixed use. Everyone talks about mixed use, but few people build it. One of the most wonderful definitions of a city ever written was by Lewis Mumford, who described it as "that place where the greatest number of activities takes place in the least amount of space." Nodding approval, we go so far as to label "central business districts" on our maps. The demise of the American downtown parallels the rise of that term, I contend. Why would anyone want to live, shop, dine, relax, meet a friend, cruise in a convertible, attend a concert, see a movie, go to school, take a walk with a sweetheart, or hang out in something called a central business district? When we permit downtowns to become mere "business districts," their appeal diminishes for everyone—even businesses themselves, which eventually leave.

Let us not pine for the return of corporations to downtown towers. Instead, let us turn our attention to overcoming the absence of all the other pleasures and places that have vanished from downtowns, whether stores, nightlife, culture, or residences. We need no longer regard mixed use as an unattainable ideal, but must, in fact, focus resources on realizing it, because a true urban mélange is what spurs excitement, growth, and revitalization—even the return of those white-collar managers to their towers. We should extend the concept of mixed use beyond offices over stores. Even some of our most remarkable early suburbs, like Forest Hills Gardens in New York, contain a rich mixture of dwelling sizes and clusters. Density in house types is more likely to accommodate density of social, economic, and age groups. Cities must overcome the unpopularity of mixing people that prevails among residential developers, who almost invariably segment populations in order to develop easy-to-build but simplistic "product."

Fear Not Design

Use beauty as a criterion, and use the eye as an instrument of urban design. Picture two streets that are about the same size—a suburban arterial and an urban boulevard. Both accommodate about the same amount of traffic, both have parking lots, and both have trees and buildings. The difference between them will have nothing to do with "old and new," although that is usually how it plays out. The difference is that one is beautiful, and the other is not. The one that attracts us is the one along which we would rather live or do business. Sometimes the best advice that a design review board can provide a mayor or a developer is simply to insist that things be more beautiful. When the Duke of Marlborough decided to renovate his estate in the early 18th century, he summoned his favorite architect, who, in a moment of modesty, said, "You must send for a landscape painter." We too often approach the city as an instrument to be engineered rather than as a place to be nurtured and designed. Beauty is a less abstract term than many used in the planning and design professions, and its useful life is far longer than yet another street widening or tax incentive. So use beauty as a criterion of town planning.

Elaborate on detail whenever possible, but especially when it affects the public environment. A little buffalo gargoyle on the face of City Hall in Buffalo, New York, is not just endearing or perhaps over the top—it places the person who stops to enjoy it in an epic of frontier urbanization. Such seemingly frivolous touches are one of the ways a sense of place is established, an aspect of urban life that endears us to it. Our public environments can benefit from more of such excess. As Mies van der Rohe said, "God rests in the details."

Build landmarks and position them well. A statue of President McKinley graces an otherwise graceless little town in western Massachusetts. In some small ways, this one statue civilizes it. The center of Riverside, Illinois, one of the early planned suburbs, has a strange little railroad station with a marvelously idiosyncratic water tower. Landmarks confer coherence, not status. Whether or not they are officially registered as historic, they earn historic status in the minds of citizens, who recognize quality and commitment when they see it. Calling a strip center "Landmark Square" or a megamall "Center Place," as developers are wont to do, does not make it so.

Rediscover the Street

Maintain a pattern of streets that is more redundant than hierarchical. Conventional traffic-engineering wisdom is to build hierarchies of streets from freeways to arterials to cul-de-sacs. But highways and multilane arterials cordon us off from each other, while remaining the source of our most frustrating traffic snarls. These regimented systems promise speed but limit choice. They are necessary on occasion, but a network of roads—even narrow and crooked ones—provides greater choice, both actual and promised. Ask any city cabbie.

Emphasize the design of the street—a lost art, I'm afraid. In a typical contemporary suburban subdivision, everything outside of the street right-of-way is carefully designed. On one side of the fence, there are beautiful houses, beautiful lawns, beautifully maintained porches, and so forth. On the other side of the fence, along the street, there is only characterless civil engineering. There is no reason that the street configuration, the curb, the sidewalk, the benches, lights, street trees, and other public furniture cannot be as carefully thought through as what's on the other side of the fence. If you want fine towns and cities, emphasize the design of the street once more.

Provide fewer—not more—parking spaces than logic dictates. This is a very important rule, even though few people yet believe it. The availability of parking is largely a psychological matter. There never seems to be enough parking no matter how much is provided, and there can't possibly ever be enough parking, because the space 20 feet closer to your destination is always preferable. This is why we have a parking problem: because the space in front of the door is always taken. By any objective measure, every American city has many more parking spaces available than cars to fill them. Providing less parking allows a clustering of activities that attracts people, who become willing to walk or take mass transit because their intended destination, and the way they get to it, is unique and interesting.

Make places worthy of walking, and pedestrians will remember that they have enjoyed the experience. Americans are known for their dislike of walking, because they are daily asked to walk hundreds of forgettable yards through desertlike parking lots, characterless shopping malls, and identically beige corridors of large buildings. It is not that Americans don't walk great distances—it is that they don't remember that they've done so, because the walking experience is a grim task. It is ironic how much of this walking is made necessary by the car. If you make places worthy of walking, you will find walkers there enjoying themselves and each other. We still need to get from point A to point B, but seductions along the path make the effort rewarding rather than a chore.

Re-use places. I am not a preservationist—there are too many preservationists. Few parts of a city warrant strict preservation, but virtually all parts of a city warrant re-use. So what we need are more re-users, people who can see the potential in an unextraordinary piece of the city that's seen better days. Unfortunately, the useful existing building is often overlooked in the zeal to build anew, somewhere else, under the dubious supposition that something new will be better. There is a tremendous movement around the country to build new "traditional" towns, like Seaside, in Florida. But there is plenty of real tradition around, looking for TLC. A few miles north of Detroit, there is a community called Southfield, which, with its freeway-entwined, could-be-anywhere shiny towers and massive malls, now boasts a daily commuting population almost as large as that coming into Detroit, which has withered. Instead of revitalizing well-built city neighborhoods, we build places like Southfield, which defines itself principally as "not Detroit." Who will love such places when they are past their prime?

Yield to privatization only with reluctance. Big downtown shopping malls, like Toronto's Eaton Center, are marvelous—perhaps the eighth wonder of the world. But you learn you are not in a truly public place when the guys in green suits throw you out for whatever they regard as misbehaving. The streets outside Eaton Center, lowly as they may be, are where you rejoin the town.

A Place for Edges, Boundaries, Greenery

Ban the term "open space." When a development touts that "forty percent of the land is devoted to open space," it is likely that forty percent of the land has been insufficiently considered. We actually have more trash-strewn setbacks, scraggly buffer strips, fetid retainage basins, and purposeless asphalted acreage—all "open space"—than we know what to do with. What we can use is more parks, natural preserves, tot lots, recreational areas, baseball fields, and football fields. If space on a development plan is labeled only open space, you don't want it.

Establish edges and define boundaries. An environment without boundary is likely placeless and indistinguishable from the amorphousness all around it. With apologies to Robert Frost, good fences may not make good neighbors, but neither does their absence foster connectivity or communality. So indeed, provide edges, as long as you also abide by the earlier-stated rule: be sure to make that edge beautiful, and something of equal value to that which is on both sides of it.

Reinstate Arbor Day as a civic holiday. Thomas Jefferson planted poplars down the great boulevards of Washington, D.C., even before any buildings had been erected there. Towards the end of the 19th century, many citizens devoted one day each year to planting trees along their city streets. Arbor Day was once a significant holiday, and it's still a good idea. Planting or maintaining street trees is one of the easiest ways we, as citizens, can improve the quality of the public environment by our own actions. Nor is it a bad way to meet your neighbors.

Zone stringently, but modify the zoning ordinance frequently. Planners and advocates of regulation confuse the need for land-use controls with their permanent applicability. Many ordinances are larded with language that is a product of long-vanished circumstances, such as the archetypal fear of the offal-spewing tannery moving onto your nice residential street. Place a mirror to your local zoning ordinance and change it if it today no longer produces the form of community its citizens desire. Don't change it by variance, overhaul it. Zone stringently to meet today's real needs, but do not be afraid to change the code as community needs change.

Do not overplan. Specifics of place, time, or desire should always be allowed to intrude into the rational process of planning. Consider Las Collinas, Texas, a new town placed midway between Dallas and Fort Worth. Nothing about this place is unplanned. The parking, the public spaces, the highway, the houses, the keys you use to get into the subdivisions, the lawnmowing schedule—all has been designed with your convenience in mind. This enormous attention and energy has failed to produce much of a community, however. Planners need to temper their instincts to organize everything and allow serendipity to intrude.

Finally, believe that design is a vehicle to change. Without design, all kinds of things will change around you, but you probably won't much like the results.

Alex Krieger, FAIA, is professor in practice of urban design and chairman of the Department of Urban Planning and Design in Harvard University's Graduate School of Design. He is a founding principal of Chan Krieger & Associates.

Design Competitions

Rosalie Genevro

Competitions, in all their various forms, are a very useful way to investigate alternative approaches and new possibilities in architecture and design. They are often used as an open-ended, explorative process—to elicit new ideas and perspectives when a building type is in flux or has become obsolete, or when an evolving form of social life has not yet become connected to a specific architectural or urban type.

Two very ambitious and fairly recent European projects suggest how complicated urban design issues can benefit from the competition process. In Ireland, a historic but dilapidated section of Dublin was slated to be demolished to make way for construction of a bus terminal. The city took years to assemble the land, and, in the interim, rented out properties at low prices to artists and other residents. This new community was committed to bettering the neighborhood and fought efforts to build the depot. Ultimately, the city agreed to hold a design competition to come up with alternatives. The competition was won by a consortium of young architects, who proposed a precise, fine-grained strategy for the entire area, in which new buildings and outdoor gathering places would be inserted at strategic points. The historic fabric would be re-used as well under new design guidelines. The community of artists and a local development corporation convinced the city to adopt this scheme, and managed the development of the project. Today Temple Bar, as the area is called, is Dublin's cultural quarter, and is

Weiss/Manfredi won a competition for Seattle's Olympic Sculpture Park by uniting a site fragmented by streets and railroad tracks with a powerful topographic form. A multi-use pavilion and plantings that reflect the diverse ecologies of the Pacific Northwest will enhance the Seattle Art Museum's rotating exhibitions. The National Endowment for the Arts helped organize the competition as part of its New Public Works program, along with local museum, private, and public sponsors.

one of the most visited tourist destinations in Europe.

Another competition of note took place in the Ruhr Valley, once the great steel-producing area of Germany but long since in decline. The area was environmentally devastated by years of heavy manufacturing and mining, followed by economic decline and high unemployment. The state government decided in the 1980s to create an "international building exposition" as a revitalization strategy. In Germany, earlier building expositions usually entailed the construction of model housing, so the focus on an abandoned manufacturing region was unusual. The Ruhr region held a number of design competitions for research-oriented business parks and to reclaim vast polluted tracts for public use. Among the competitions was one for a park called Landscape Park Duisberg North, which was won by the Munich-based landscape architect Peter Latz. Latz proposed to leave the industrial installations in place as ruins and to interweave them with newly designed public landscapes. Designed to be installed over several years, the park has groves of trees that help purify the toxic soil, and a public plaza called Piazza Metallica, which is paved with large steel plates scavenged from buildings. Local diving teams practice in former storage tanks, now filled with water, while other salvaged fragments were used to make a "rock" climbing wall. The park has become extremely popular with surrounding communities.

The lesson of competitions is that they are not simply a way to solve a particular problem but can also be excellent public-education tools. They serve as collective investigative enterprises. Architects benefit because they get a chance to explore ideas, sites, and conditions. The process also benefits the public by informing and engaging interested citizens and affected people alike. At their best, competitions make the ground more fertile for design's highest aspirations. The best competitions raise awareness of the relationship between design and the life of communities.

Rosalie Genevro is the executive director of the Architectural League of New York.

Top:
Prequalified firms from across the country were invited to compete for the renovation and expansion of the Booker T. Washington High School for the Performing and Visual Arts, in Dallas' Arts District. Allied Works, a Portland, Oregon, architect, won with a proposal that fit the large addition on a limited site by wrapping new wings around a courtyard.

Bottom:
Blocklike forms catch the sharp western light and evoke the nearby Wasatch Range in the Utah Museum of Fine Arts, in Salt Lake City, Utah. The competition-winning design is by Machado and Silvetti Associates, of Boston, with the local firm of Prescott Muir Architects.

Community Workshops

James S. Russell

Design workshops, also known as charettes, have risen to prominence in recent years because they take a positive view of the role citizens can play in design. There are a variety of ways to structure workshops, but they share common qualities. They are a way to involve interested citizens in defining the criteria for a project, in understanding and evaluating the tradeoffs that public projects entail, and may even result in sketches that can form the basis for a design. Workshops involve citizens more directly, asking them to identify key issues, make choices about scenarios, and consider alternatives in much the same way designers and public officials do. Public agencies can run workshops during the early stages of a project to test program criteria or to gauge the issues that most concern the public. By being proactive, the integrity of the project planning can be better maintained and is less likely to be derailed at a late stage by a failure to identify important concerns.

A charette is a type of workshop used to define important issues and envision the future. Participants meet intensively for two or three days to define criteria that apply to a project, then go through a testing, design, and sketching process that may result in alternative approaches to a design. The sponsor need not create the expectation that the result of a charette is binding as a design document. Technical or cost criteria, for example, cannot be fully explored in such a fast-paced process involving so many nonexperts. But participants in the process come out with a deep

It may look like a board game, but the hands-on workshops run by SMWM help people come to terms with conflicting desires for a miles-long swath of new land in the middle of the city. It will be made available by the Central Artery Project (known locally in Boston as the "big dig"), which routes parts of two interstate highways underground. The process turns talk into engagement: acquainting people with the issues at stake and helping them see the full range of possibilities.

117

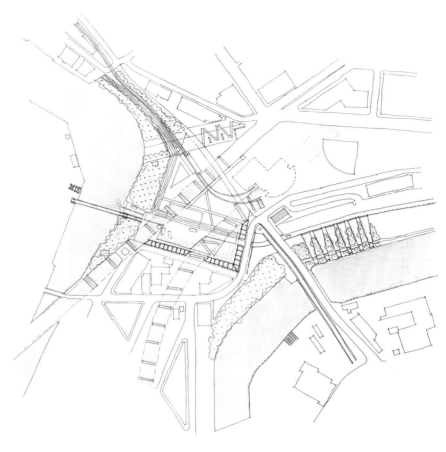

commitment to solving problems through design—as well as a deep appreciation for the complexity of the design process.

Though citizens can be given a voice in public hearings, workshops offer a means of communication that is often more satisfying and more effective at identifying issues and assigning them a priority. While workshop participants express their concerns, they also gain an understanding of the factors that drive a project. When citizens are involved in exercises whose purpose is to reconcile a variety of interests, they come to appreciate the importance of consensus and the need for compromise. In this way, workshops often defuse controversy and help build a constituency for important projects.

These sketches were drawn as part of a charette to envision a possible Canal Basin Park, in Cleveland, Ohio. Sketches by Ignacio Bunster-Ossa and Sylvia Palms, of WRT, suggest how to integrate public recreation with the powerful forms of the city's industrial heritage. It was undertaken by the Cleveland Urban Design Collaborative, a community-oriented design center operated by Kent State University.

Biographies

Image Credits

Biographies

James S. Russell is editor-at-large at *Architectural Record* magazine, the premier American journal for practicing architects and the magazine of the American Institute of Architects. He writes on a variety of design, construction-technology, and professional practice topics for the magazine. He also contributes articles on architecture and design to numerous other books, exhibitions, and publications, including the *New York Times*, the *Philadelphia Inquirer*, *I.D.*, the *Harvard Design Magazine*, *Business Week*, *Details*, and *Grid*. He teaches at Columbia University's Graduate School of Architecture, Planning & Preservation.

Mr. Russell was a staff editor at *Architectural Record* for 10 years, where he rose from associate editor to managing senior editor. During that time he pioneered coverage of infrastructure, the design of the workplace, and urban-design stories rarely touched-on by design publications. His work has helped the magazine earn two Jesse Neal Awards and two McGraw-Hill Corporate Achievement awards.

Before joining *Architectural Record*, Mr. Russell practiced architecture with firms in New York City, Philadelphia, and Seattle. He is a registered architect in New York and a member of the American Institute of Architects. He is active with the Architectural League and the Municipal Arts Society, in New York.

Mr. Russell earned a Master of Architecture degree from Columbia University and a Bachelor of Arts in Environmental Design degree from the University of Washington. He also attended the Evergreen State College. He was born in Seattle and resides in New York City.

Christine Saum, AIA, has been the Executive Director of the Mayors' Institute on City Design since 1993. Through her work with the MICD, Ms. Saum has visited cities across the country to help their mayors prepare for Institute sessions, and she has continued to work with them following their participation as they implement the lessons they learned.

Ms. Saum has also administered Leadership Initiatives in design at the National Endowment for the Arts. One was the Federal Design Improvement Program (with the Public Building Service of the General Services Administration), which promotes design excellence in public buildings. Another was the Federal Properties Conversion Initiative, which sponsored a series of public design workshops in Monterey County, California, concerned with the redevelopment of Fort Ord.

Ms. Saum received a Bachelor of Fine Arts in Interior Design from Virginia Commonwealth University in Richmond and a Master of Architecture from The Catholic University of America in Washington, D.C. A registered architect and interior designer, she practiced interior architecture in Nashville and in Washington, D.C., for more than 10 years. She is a charter member of the Congress for the New Urbanism and served as an advisor to the American Architectural Foundation on the development of *Back from the Brink: Saving America's Cities by Design*—a public television program broadcast nationally. She writes and lectures on how the design process can unite with political leadership to promote community livability. She lives in Washington, D.C.

Mark Robbins is the Director of Design at the National Endowment for the Arts where he has undertaken an aggressive program to strengthen the presence of design in the public realm. In addition to efforts to expand grant opportunities he has instituted new Leadership Initiatives including New Public Works, which supports national design competitions. Collectively, these activities have doubled the available funding for the Endowment's design-related activities.

His work encompasses architecture, installations, exhibitions, and teaching. He has received awards including the Prix de Rome from the American Academy in Rome and fellowships from the New York Foundation for the Arts, the National Endowment for the Arts, and the Graham Foundation for Advanced Studies in the Fine Arts. Before coming to Washington in 1999, Mr. Robbins was an Associate Professor in the Knowlton School of Architecture at The Ohio State University. In addition, he was Curator of Architecture at the Wexner Center for the Arts from 1993 to 1999.

Image Credits

12 (#1): Courtesy of Machado and Silvetti Associates, photo © Michael Moran

12 (#2): Courtesy of Sasaki Associates, Inc.

12 (#3): Courtesy of New York City Department of Cultural Affairs, Percent for Art program (1999)

12 (#4): Courtesy of Saint Paul Riverfront Corporation

12 (#5): Courtesy of Skidmore, Owings & Merrill LLP

20: © Sony Development, Inc., 1999, photo by Timothy Hursley

22–23 (#1–2): Photos © Timothy Hursley

22–23 (#3): Photo © Timothy Hursley

22–23 (#4): Courtesy of New Jersey Performing Arts Center

24: Courtesy of Rob Wellington Quigley Architecture/Planning, photo by Brighton Noing

26–27 (#1): Courtesy of Hargreaves Associates, photo by John Gollings

26–27 (#2): Courtesy of D.I.R.T. Studio, photo by Thomas Woltz, Nelson-Byrd Landscape Architects

26–27 (#3): Courtesy of White River State Park, photo © Banayote Photography, Inc.

26–27 (#4): Courtesy of the American Museum of Natural History, photo by Denis Finnin

26–27 (#5): Photo courtesy of Balthazar Korab

31: Courtesy of Alexander Cooper Associates (1979)

32–33 (#1): Courtesy of Myers Schmalenberger/MSI

32–33 (#2–3): Courtesy of Hargreaves Associates, illustrations by Christopher Grubbs

36–37 (#1, #3): Graphics prepared by Michael Gallis & Associates © 2002

36–37 (#2): Courtesy of Moule & Polyzoides, Architects and Urbanists

36–37 (#4): Courtesy of Wallace Roberts & Todd, LLC

40 (top): Courtesy of Stanley Saitowitz Office, photo by Stanley Saitowitz

40 (bottom): Courtesy of Phoenix Arts Commission, Percent for Art program, photo by Craig Smith (2000)

42 (#1–4): Courtesy of New York City Department of Cultural Affairs, Percent for Art program (1992)

42 (#5–6): Courtesy of New York City Department of Cultural Affairs, Percent for Art program (1998)

54–55 (#1): Courtesy of Peter Walker and Partners, photo by Alan Ward

54–55 (#2): Courtesy of Ken Kay Associates

54–55 (#3): Photo © Felice Frankel for Olin Partnership

54–55 (#4): Courtesy of Wallace Roberts & Todd, LLC, photo by Tim Street-Porter

56–57 (#2): Courtesy of Miller/Hull Partnership LLP, photo by Art Grice

58–59 (#2): Courtesy of Machado and Silvetti Associates, photo © Michael Moran

58–59 (#3): Photo © Timothy Hursley

60–61 (#1): Courtesy of Stanley Saitowitz Office, photo by Steven Rosenthal

60–61 (#2): Courtesy of Loom, photo by Christian Faust

60–61 (#3): Courtesy of James Cutler Architects, photo by James Cutler

62, 68–69 (2): © SOM / Steinkamp/Ballogg Photography

68–69 (#1): Courtesy of Selbert Perkins Design

68–69 (3): Courtesy of Center City Development, photo by Skip Jurus

68–69 (#4–5): Courtesy of ROMA Design Group, photos by Bob Swanson (garden) and Ira Kahn (aerial)

70: Photo © Rod Berry

78–79 (#1–2): Courtesy of MGA Partners Architects, photos by Perretti & Park Pictures

78–79 (#3): Photo © Richard Benjamin

78–79 (#4): Courtesy of and photo by James Russell

80: Photo © Timothy Hursley

86–87 (#1): Courtesy of Hargreaves Associates

86–87 (#2): Courtesy of Phoenix Arts Commission, Percent for Art program, photo by David Stansbury

86–87 (#3): Photo © JoAnn Sieburg-Baker

86–87 (#4): Courtesy of Miller/Hull Partnership, photo by James Housel
88, 92–93 (#2): Courtesy of David Baker + Partners, photo by Brian Rose

92–93 (#1): Courtesy of Studio A, Inc., photo by Dickson Dunlap

92–93 (#3): Courtesy of Koning Eizenberg, photo by Grant Mudford (1998)

92–93 (#4) Courtesy of Goody, Clancy & Associates, Inc., photo by Steve Rosenthal (1991)

Image Credits (continued)

92–93 (#5) Courtesy of Studio E
Architects

94, 100–1 (#3): Courtesy of Ken
Kay Associates

100–1 (#1): Courtesy of Wallace
Roberts & Todd, LLC

100–1 (#2): Courtesy of Michael
Van Valkenburgh Associates, Inc.,
photo by Ed Massery (2000)

100–1 (#4–5): Courtesy of
Hargreaves Associates, photos by
John Gollings

104: © SOM / Steinkamp/Ballogg
Photography

112: Courtesy of Weiss/Manfredi
Architects

115 (top): Courtesy of Allied Works
Architecture

115 (bottom): Courtesy of Machado
and Silvetti Associates, photo
© Michael Moran

117: Courtesy of SMWM Planning

118: Illustrations © Ignacio
Bunster, Wallace Roberts & Todd,
LLC